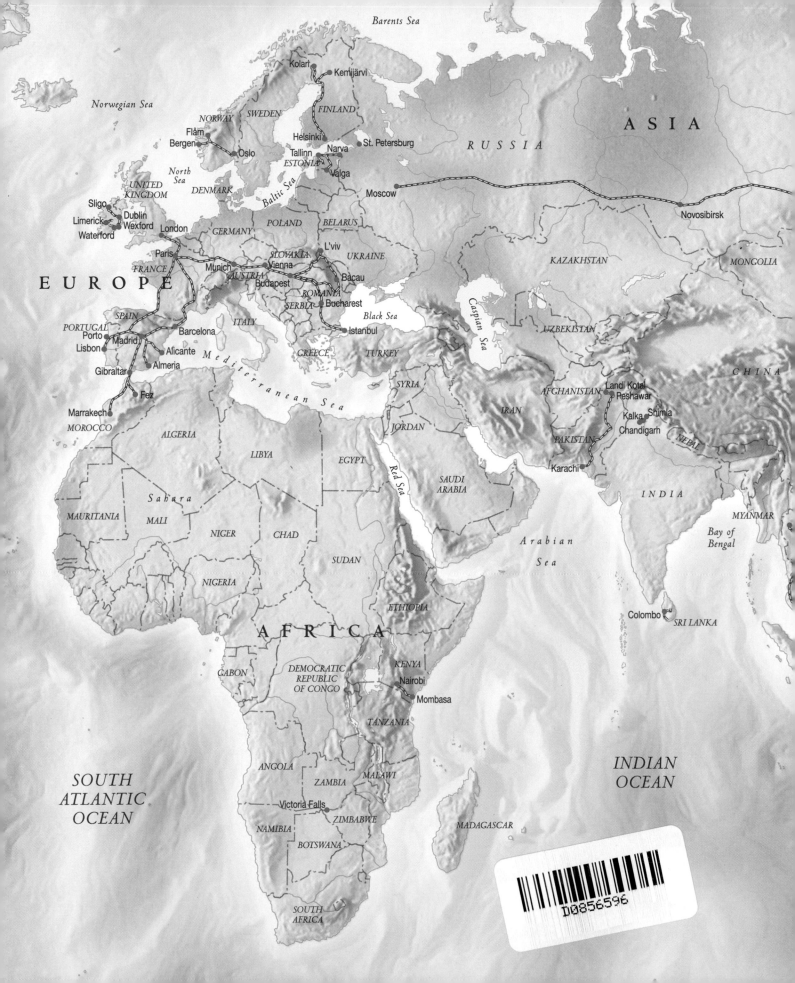

THE WORLD'S MOST EXOTIC
RAILWAY JOURNEYS

50 of the most dramatic, scenic and long-distance routes across the globe

Dedication

To the Members of the Irish Railway Record Society who
have travelled far and wide in search of interesting railways.

These pages: Since its rediscovery in 1911, Peru's Machu Picchu has
become one the world's most visited archeological sites. The best way to
reach the site is by train.

Previous page: The West Coast Wilderness Train in Tasmania, Australia,
is hauled by an Abt rack and pinion engine.

THE WORLD'S MOST EXOTIC
RAILWAY JOURNEYS

50 of the most dramatic, scenic and long-distance routes across the globe

BRIAN SOLOMON
with contributions from Paul Bigland, David Bowden and Scott Lothes

Jb

JOHN BEAUFOY PUBLISHING

CONTENTS

Opposite: PeruRail trains operate several daily round trips on the narrow gauge line between Machu Picchu and Cusco (Poroy).

INTRODUCTION

This book explores a fascinating variety of the world's most exotic railways. But what is 'exotic'? For some travellers a line operating at the furthest corners of the globe from their home seems exotic, while many readers may be fascinated by any colourful journey beyond their own travel limits, and for others a line that rarely operates qualifies. The railwayman who regularly runs a train on a lightly used branch line in the hinterlands finds nothing exotic in his daily chore; the commuter faced with the same journey, back and forth on a daily basis, isn't fascinated by his travels, yet a visitor from thousands of miles away, might delight in each and every twist of that very line.

An exotic railway journey may include views rarely seen, or isolated and exceptional scenery, plus the chance to experience different cultures and meet new people. It may provide the opportunity to travel on distinctive, antique or otherwise noteworthy railway equipment along with the possibility of riding over interesting trackage or unusual infrastructure. While some travellers desire luxurious accommodation on special first-class trains outfitted with all the best amenities, others seek out more unassuming trips on an unusual backwater branch line with only basic carriages.

Rail travel in the developing world has undergone many changes in recent decades. Many of the journeys once enjoyed by adventurous railway enthusiasts, especially those in Africa, Central and South America and the Middle East are no longer possible. Economic and political changes have resulted in the closing of regular passenger operations, or, even where some semblance of service is maintained, have made travelling by train virtually impossible for foreign visitors. Through the 1980s Mexico, for example, offered a range of remarkable railway trips. Today, except for a handful of trains, most remaining Mexican railways are devoid of regular passenger service. Thus some of the routes described in the book are conceptual; they are no longer possible as a single trip.

International long-distance trains have also suffered. Political difficulties, low-cost airlines and the continued proliferation of highway transport have taken their toll. Branch lines, long the favourite of railway explorers, have suffered terribly. When a nation faces a budget crisis, branch lines are often the first sacrificial lambs. Even nations with well-developed rail services are quick to target branch-line trains when money becomes tight. Never assume that just because a branch is listed in the timetable today, it will be running tomorrow. However, tourist railways have flourished in many areas, and these offer excursions on a variety of scenic and exotic routes. In many areas suburban railways and domestic intercity lines enjoy steady and growing ridership.

The mechanics of planning a trip have also changed since, with the advent of the internet and its online resources, many railways have discontinued the tradition of the paper timetable. The ability to check train times online is a fantastic resource, yet navigating internet browsers can be frustrating and counterintuitive. Often the browser assumes travellers know where they are going, and websites are ill-suited to the casual perusal of schedules that traditionally allowed for planning of exotic trips. Even the staples of exotic travel, such as Thomas Cook's Overseas Timetable, that were a rich source for the curious and those organizing their own travel, have been discontinued. Scouring the internet may yield some of the benefits of the paper timetable, and in theory can produce up-to-date information, but in practice internet searches can be vastly more time consuming than the quick reference once available in Cook's, and too often conceal the very information that the intrepid traveller is hoping to find!

Nevertheless, many of the world's most celebrated railroad journeys, while distant, can be comparatively easy to plan. Tour companies and train operators facilitate holiday travel. Tour operator Belmond, with its flagship *Venice Simplon-Orient-Express*, continues to offer a variety of classy, high-end, railway-themed excursions over popular routes. Railways in many countries operate regularly scheduled services and while a great many of these may not once have been deemed exotic, some meet the criteria listed here, including infrequent service on branch lines, overnight trains across rural mountain passes and journeys across national boundaries.

For the most adventurous railway travellers, there are options beyond scheduled services. Charters can be arranged and individual travellers can sometimes make their own opportunities. For example, the view from the cab of a locomotive is one of the best on any railway, but it is rarely advertised and often officially off-limits to ordinary passengers. When the only train that travels a lonely exotic route is the occasional maintenance train, it helps to make friends with the train crew. These can be the most rewarding experiences and the friends you make in a locomotive cab can stay with you for a lifetime.

For the traveller desiring comfort and luxury, it's best to stay with the advertised deluxe services, but for the intrepid railway enthusiast aiming to seek out the world's most interesting railways, details such as creature comforts are secondary to the experience. For both types of traveller, this book is a guide and a source of inspiration. A word of caution for those wish to travel on a certain railway, don't wait! You never know when unforeseen events may shut a line forever or otherwise make the journey impossible. In railway travel, nothing is ever certain.

Brian Solomon

Above: Belmond's Venice Simplon-Orient-Express *traverses the Swiss Alps using the Lotschberg Pass. Here the train is seen descending towards Brig.*

These pages: Russia's Trans-Siberian Railway is a heavily travelled freight corridor that also hosts the world's longest railway journeys. Electric locomotives lead a coal train on a sinuous portion of the route in the Primorsky-region of far-eastern Siberia.

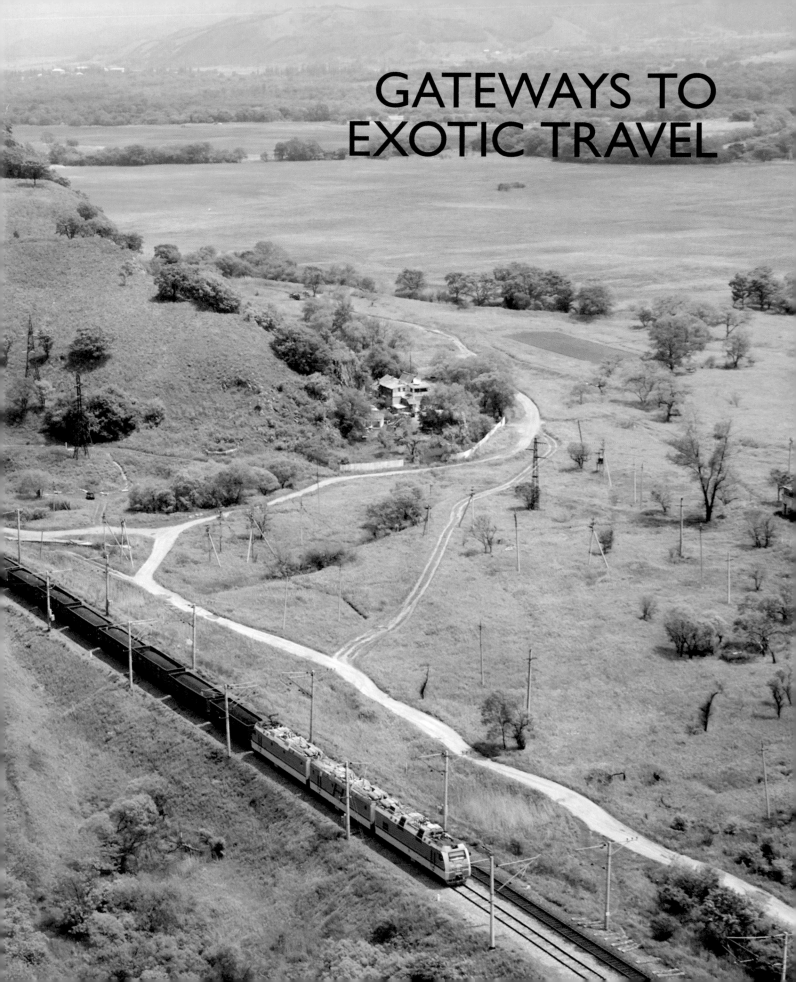

GATEWAYS TO
EXOTIC TRAVEL

THE *ORIENT EXPRESS*: PARIS TO ISTANBUL
In the Path of Europe's Most Famous Train

BRIAN SOLOMON

Europe's *Orient Express* remains among the world's most famous trains, its mystique glorified by literature and film, and its route shrouded by changes to the political map. Yet while high-end tour trains have adopted its name and offer an element of the classic style often associated with the *Orient Express*, the train in its purest form hasn't operated in decades.

The casual armchair traveller frequently confuses the *Orient Express* with Russia's Trans-Siberian route, perhaps because many trans-Siberian travellers journey from Europe to China. There are several important distinctions. Where the *Orient Express* was a service that used several different routes via various lines over more than a century, the Trans-Siberian is a railway route that has hosted myriad trains. At no point did any of the *Orient Express* trains come anywhere near the Trans-Siberian route. In its original incarnation, the *Orient Express* was a service connecting Paris, Vienna, Budapest and Istanbul; while the Trans-Siberian is a railway running east from Moscow to the Pacific port of Vladivostok, with various connections to lines elsewhere in Asia.

One of the Historic Routes of Wagon-Lits Orient Express

Another common misconception is the use of the term 'Orient.' To the Victorian traveller, the 'Orient' had a very different meaning than it has today. It inferred countries to the 'east' of western Europe. In Roman times, the Eastern Empire included 'Orient' in its description and referred essentially to the Balkans. For a Victorian-era tourist, the Balkans represented an exotic region on the periphery of Europe where peasants in colourful costumes made for an unusual and titillating travel experience. Constantinople was the gateway to Asia on the Bosphorus, and was the seat of the Ottoman Empire. Today, 'Orient' tends to mean the Far East, which was beyond the horizon as far as railway travellers from Paris were concerned in the late 19th century.

Wagons-Lits

In the 19th century, the lack of integration between railways of different European nations made travelling between countries a difficult and arduous process. These difficulties led Belgian entrepreneur Georges Nagelmackers to innovate a solution involving the provision of sleeping cars or *wagons-lits*. What is often forgotten is that his inspiration came from riding Pullman, sleeping-car trains in the United States, which at that time provided a comparatively good service between major cities. Nagelmackers was a fortunate man: the son of a wealthy banker and a trained engineer who had travelled widely. Nagelmackers' organization, Compagnie Internationale des Wagons-Lits, offered what no other railway service in Europe was prepared to do: cross-border luxury travel, thus greatly simplifying the business of travelling between countries, especially for wealthy travellers with lots of luggage. He combined the concept of steam-ship convenience and comfort with the speed and service of the railway. Over the years, Wagons-Lits expanded greatly across Europe and operated a host of deluxe international services, of which *Orient Express* remained one of the best known.

Above and opposite: Compagnie Internationale des Wagon-Lits advertised comfort and travel to exotic destinations. The Paris-Istanbul Express d'Orient was their best-known train. In its heyday this carried wealthy and influential travellers across the Balkans to the Ottoman capital.

The exotic imagery conveyed by travelling east from Paris was very compelling, so much so that it continued to sell Wagons-Lits' *Orient Express* for decades. For the purist, the true *Orient Express* died with the onset of the First World War, yet the train, in name and in spirit, was revived again and again over the years. When the smoke of war had cleared, a new service named the *Simplon-Orient-Express* was installed on a southerly route through France, Switzerland, northern Italy and the recently created Yugoslavia, totally avoiding German and Austrian territory while taking advantage of the recently opened Swiss Simplon Tunnel

route through the Alps. This train followed a completely new route between end points running via Milan, Venice, Trieste, Zagreb and Belgrade, before continuing to Istanbul (the official new name for Constantinople after the founding of the modern Turkish state in 1922).

During the 1920s, rebuilding of German and Austrian lines allowed Wagons-Lits to resume a more traditional *Orient Express* routing, as well as a trans-Alpine service over the Arlberg Pass in Austria called the *Arlberg-Orient Express*, which began in 1932. The Second World War caused Wagons-Lits to suspend service for a number of years. By the 1960s Cold War tensions effectively truncated the train at Vienna, eliminating the most exotic portion of the journey. Although it carried the *Orient Express* name, the train appeared little different from most other European intercity express trains. The *Orient Express* name survived into the mid-2000s but had none of the panache of its historic antecedent.

Above: Today the Venice Simplon-Orient-Express cruise train emulates the classic styles of the 1920s and 1930s on its vintage trains.

Venice Simplon-Orient-Express

Travellers desiring to relive the spirit of Wagons-Lits deluxe European train travel, will delight in the classic luxury cruise train offered by the *Venice Simplon-Orient-Express* operated by Belmond. VSOE is operated as a 16-carriage train consisting of former Wagons-Lits equipment. Most of these are from the inter-war period. The carriages are painted in the traditional cream and navy, with wonderfully restored interiors, opulently finished in plush fabric, varnished wooden panels and highly polished metal fixtures.

This is advertised as a romantic London/Paris-Venice, Pullman-style, two-day one-night excursion. The route requires two sets of equipment, which has historical precedents. Passengers board a restored British Pullman train at London's Victoria Station and ride to the Kentish coast where they transfer to a ferry. Upon arriving on the continent, they board another VSOE train, equipped for the overnight run to Italy. Typically, VSOE's train runs from Calais, France, southwards via the Gare de l'Est in Paris, then east through Switzerland and south to Verona, Italy, and finally Venice. While a stunning journey in either direction, travellers seem to prefer the southbound run.

An alternate routing boards at Bruges, Belgium and runs via Germany. Belmond also offers what it calls a 'Signature Journey' that more closely follows the route of Nagelmackers' 1883 inaugural train, working from Paris to Budapest and Istanbul. This is a six-day, five-night trip, and may only operate once a year. For all of Belmond's VSOE trains, passengers must pre-book accommodation.

Opposite: After the First World War, the Express d'Orient route through Germany and Austria was temporarily replaced with the Simplon-Orient-Express using a southerly route via France, through Switzerland on the recently completed Bern Lotschberg-Simplon line to Italy and beyond. It is this route that the modern-day Venice Simplon-Orient-Express emulates.

Tracing the Route of the old Orient Express

In the 1880s, Nagelmackers' original train began at Gare de l'Est in Paris, working twice weekly across central Europe towards Turkey. France's Compagnie de l'Est hosted it to Alsace-Lorraine (territory then under the administration of the German authorities). It continued on various German state railways via Karlsruhe and Stuttgart, up the Geislingen incline and across the Bavarian plains to Munich. Once in the Hapsburg domains, it travelled via Salzburg, Vienna and Budapest. East of Budapest the route changed a number of times as improved means of reaching the Bosphorus were devised.

Although it has been many years since you could board a scheduled passenger train at Gare de l'Est with a direct run to Istanbul, it's still possible to travel this route via scheduled first-class services while experiencing the overnight portions in a sleeping car. Although you have to change trains, the service is much quicker than in Victorian times. At its inception, the original route required a 75-hour journey (and that was considered vastly quicker than earlier options). Today, with train changes you can make the trip in just 58 hours.

Begin on a Sunday, having enjoyed a full day in Paris exploring the city's riches and wonders. Perhaps a few hours in The Louvre on the right bank of the Seine. Or for those who like to blend railway interest with art appreciation, a visit to the Museé d'Orsay, which began as the Gare d'Orsay, a main station on the Paris—Orléans railway. Maybe a visit to the Eiffel Tower, or a spin out on the RER suburban lines to Louis XIV's palace at Versailles. Take your time to dine in Paris before you board, as there's no formal diner on the train, although snacks and

Left: Historically Wagons-Lits' Orient Express departed from Paris Gare de l'Est. Although the train no longer operates, the old station remains well used by less evocative services.

small meals are available, then make your way to Gare de l'Est, one of Paris' six main railway terminals. It is adjacent to Gare du Nord (terminus for the *Eurostar* and Thalys high-speed trains). Be sure to pre-book your tickets for the City Night Line 'hotel train' for München (Munich), as reservations are mandatory. The train departs platform 13 at 8 p.m. sharp and runs overnight to the Bavarian capital following much of the same route as the old *Orient Express*.

The tracks and equipment have been much improved since Georges Nagelmackers' original train and you'll glide along in modern comfort, if not Victorian opulence. Overnight you'll cross the German frontier and travel via one of the steepest mainlines in Germany east of Stuttgart, the famed Geislingen incline (1 in 44.5), and beyond via the historic city of Ulm. The days of pausing for a steam banking engine to assist have long since passed, and today the route is completely electrified.

You'll arrive at the busy München Hauptbahnhof just after 7 a.m. and will have a leisurely 2 hours and 20 minutes to change trains. Take the time for breakfast in one of the station restaurants. Just before 9.30 a.m., you'll depart on the RailJet (RJ63) for Budapest via Salzburg and Vienna. This is a fine train

Above: At the top of the Geislingen incline on the German section of the route; the watershed between the Rhine and the Danube.

and the scenery is splendid. On the way to Wien (Vienna) you'll follow the Danube valley. While portions of the original line are used, modern upgrades have straightened Austrian Westbahn into a modern transportation raceway. The run between Vienna and Budapest follows a traditional route.

The RailJet serves Budapest Keleti (East Station), the most interesting of the Hungarian capital's main railway terminals, which features a vast train shed with a characteristic fan-shaped front window (see page 165). This was a traditional break

Above: An Austrian Federal Railways CityShuttle rolls along the Danube east of Ybbs on the route used by the old Orient Express.

Opposite: A Deutsche Bahn ICE train is seen at the bottom of the famous Geislingen incline.

point for the *Orient Express* and conveys a feeling of adventurous travel. As you work your way further and further east, the differences between western and eastern Europe will become readily apparent.

At Budapest you change to a EuroNight train (EN473) which departs just after 7 p.m. This has more in common with traditional overnight trains of the mid-20th century than the overly sanitized City Night Line. However, Hungarian first-class trains are generally of a high standard and this one is scheduled to carry a restaurant car, so plan for dinner on the train. The journey over the Hungarian plains east of Budapest is conducted in darkness, but you'll ride in daylight over the Transylvanian Alps (otherwise known as the Southern Carpathians), territory famous for the birthplace of Vlad Tepes, the vicious medieval lord who inspired Bram Stoker's Dracula. If your imagination is ripe you can take an imaginary trip following the trail of Stoker's Jonathan Harker on his journey from London to meet Count Dracula. (The story begins with Harker's train ride.)

At Bucureşti Nord (Bucharest North Station) you'll face a tight connection with a Romanian fast train that carries through sleepers to Istanbul. Only 20 minutes is allowed, and depending on the timeliness of your train from Budapest, the wise traveller will waste no time changing from one to the other.

You depart Bucharest at 12.30 p.m. and travel via Bulgaria and western Turkey for arrival at Istanbul Sirkeci just before 8 a.m. the next morning. Having departed Paris on a Sunday night, you'll have arrived on a Wednesday morning and will have travelled through seven nations. Although no longer an opulent through run, this remains one of the world's great railway journeys.

LONDON TO IBERIA AND BEYOND
Gateway to North Africa

BRIAN SOLOMON

A dedicated railway traveller will shun other modes of transport whenever it is possible to take the train. The reasons may vary, but ground transport is preferable to air, rail preferable to road, and, where water must be

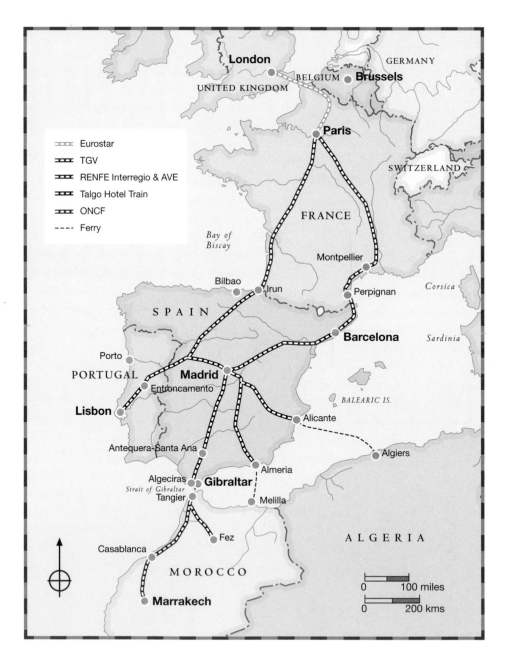

crossed, a ship is preferable to plane. In the days of low-cost airlines, rarely does an all-rail or a rail-sail journey enjoy either a speed or cost advantage, but it does allow the traveller a more timely experience. A train, even a high-speed train, gives the traveller a better sense of distance, terrain, climate and how places differ from one another.

Today, many international railway journeys have become more difficult as a result of political, economic and modal changes. Yet, the expansion of European high-speed railway networks and the opening of the Channel Tunnel in 1994, have made it easier to embark on all-rail journeys from cities in the United Kingdom to mainland Europe. Prior to this, passengers bound for the continent needed to take a ferry across the English Channel.

All-rail journeys from Paris to Spain and Portugal have been possible since the 19th century. A popular option for crossing the French-Spanish frontier was between Hendaye and Irun, where the gauge difference between Iberian lines and French railways usually meant that passengers changed trains. Wagon-Lits' luxurious *Sud Express* travelled this way from Paris to Madrid and Lisbon. Before the First World War this was deemed one of the world's most comfortable trains. In the 1950s, the Madrid-Irun route was among the first routes equipped with modern, streamlined, lightweight trains manufactured by TALGO (a Spanish company) that expedited schedules. In more recent times, gauge-changing TALGO trains have made through operations between Barcelona and south-eastern France and beyond to Switzerland possible.

In the 1990s, Spain imported the French high-speed railway technology, and built all-new high-speed lines to connect its most important cities; these routes initially hosted specially styled TGV-like trains (*Trains à Grand Vitesse*), marketed as *Alta Velocidad Española* (AVE). Significantly, the Spanish AVE uses the continental track gauge. In 2010, France and Spain's high-speed railway networks were finally linked. Today, you can board a high-speed train in London and travel all the way to a variety of Iberian destinations, although this still requires several train changes en route.

Begin in London at the magnificently transformed St Pancras International terminal, where the Victorian, balloon-style, iron train-shed and fabulously ornate Grand Midland Hotel have been integrated into a multi-tier transportation

Above: The opening of the Channel Tunnel in 1994 connected London directly by rail with the continent. Initially, Eurostar trains were routed to an International Terminal at Waterloo Station, but in 2007 the recently transformed St Pancras debuted as London's international terminal. St Pancras features the first balloon-style train shed, a design credited to R. M. Ordish, and built by the Butterley Company of Derbyshire. The Victorian shed makes a dramatic contrast to modern high-speed Eurostar cross-channel trains.

hub. From here, *Eurostar* high-speed trains depart regularly for both Brussels and Paris. These trains travel at speeds of up to 186 mph (300 kph) which allows for a travel time of just under two-and-a-half hours to Paris Gare du Nord. The next leg is probably the most difficult, transiting Paris on the Métro which can take an hour or more to reach Gare de Lyon, where a TGV departs for Barcelona. This train makes a six-and-a-half hour sprint down through France and across the Spanish frontier. Another train change is required at Barcelona and from there it is now just three-and-a-half hours on the Spanish AVE to Madrid.

Historically, Spanish railways shared the 5 foot 6 inch (1,676 mm) track gauge with their Iberian neighbour, Portugal, which facilitated through train operation. Over the years various gateways between the two countries saw through rail service. Although cross-border service between Spain and Portugal is a shadow of what it once was, it is still possible to make the journey on scheduled trains, and to do so in comfort. An overnight hotel train using TALGO low-profile cars departs Madrid-Chamartin in the evening for an early morning arrival in Lisbon.

Another option is to travel by TGV from Paris Montparnasse to Irun, then board the *Sud Express*, a TALGO hotel train that runs directly to Lisbon, although service is less frequent on this route.

Consider an even bolder adventure. Travel from London to Barcelona, then via AVE to Antequera-Santa Ana where you change for an 'Interregio' train to Algeciras to board a ferry and sail across the Straits of Gibraltar to Tangier in Morocco. Alternatively, Spanish trains from Madrid will bring you to Alicante, Almeria or Malaga, which also offer ferry services to North African destinations in Morocco and Algeria. To explore Morocco by rail, Morocco's national railway, Office National des Chemins de Fer du Maroc (ONCF), operates a modern passenger network with trains running from Tangier to Casablanca, Marrakech and Fez, among other destinations.

Below: The nightly Lisbon – Madrid hotel train pauses at Entroncamento, Portugal. Both Iberian mainline networks use broad gauge tracks which permit easy interchange between them.

THE TRANS-SIBERIAN RAILWAY
The World's Longest Railway

BRIAN SOLOMON

The Trans-Siberian journey is *the* big one. Its great length and immense scope have long made it the top pilgrimage of world travellers and railway enthusiasts. It is a journey that many people hope to take before their final hour. For those who have, they wear it like a batch of honour.

The Trans-Siberian is far more than just one train on one line. It consists of several interconnected routes that can be taken in any number of ways. The original Trans-Siberian route was built in Tsarist times to connect Moscow and the Pacific port of Vladivostok. Construction commenced in 1892 from both ends. The line was finally opened in 1905, and contributed to the taming and settling of the wild Siberian lands. Today, the core Trans-Siberian route is a fully electrified, double-track line that serves as a trunk line in the Russian railway network. It is a heavily travelled freight route, a passenger life-line for myriad communities along the way as well as an ever-popular route for tourists and travellers.

The classic approach is to begin the journey in Moscow and travel the length of Russia, 5,777 miles (9,297 km), on the appropriately named *Rossiya* to Vladivostok. This trip takes seven days and six nights. One traveller described Vladivostok as 'like San Francisco without glamour'. The journey can be made in reverse, although going from west to east is the more common choice.

Interestingly, while few railway travellers write of making a round trip across Russia, railway-travel purists frown on flying to Trans-Siberian terminal cities to begin the journey and advocate travelling overland from London, Paris or other European railway hubs, while also continuing the rail journey at the eastern end. Popular alternatives to the all-Russian journey, are the Trans-Manchurian and Trans-Mongolian options, where the Siberian leg of the trip terminates in China, with Beijing being a common destination for both routes (see pages 30 to 33).

In Soviet times, Vladivostok was closed to foreigners, owing to its importance as a naval base. Instead foreign travellers were directed to Nakhodka via a branch off the main Trans-Siberian route from Ussunysk. An alternative route across eastern Siberia is via the 'Second Trans-Siberian' railway, the once-elusive BAM line (although rarely spelled out, this stands for Baikal-Amur-Magistral) that runs to the north of the original route, deviating near Tayshet (2,810 miles/4,522 km east of Moscow) and terminating at the Pacific port of Sovetskaya Gavan.

Above: Most recognizable of Moscow's architecture is St Basil's Cathedral on Red Square. Finished in 1561, it is a legacy of Russia's Ivan the Terrible. Many Trans-Siberian tourists begin with a visit to Moscow before embarking on their eastward sojourn across the seemingly endless taiga.

Siberia

The Trans-Siberian railway was built in an effort to develop and better extract the region's resources. The railway was a life-line, but also a conduit for the exploitation of Russia's natural wealth, in much the same way that America's Trans-Continental railroads were. In Soviet times, a trip on the Trans-Siberian offered a window on a society shaped by communism and largely closed to Western visitors. The mystique the Soviet Union conveyed was the lure that attracted many visitors. Siberia was a place that Russians endured, but Westerners visited.

Gorbachev's rule brought an end to the old regime. No longer are blue jeans coveted currency. The Russian economy has opened to western investment, and business has poked its nose all over Siberia. Yet everything isn't necessarily what it seems. The trip on the Trans-Siberian still seems to be a key to that elusive viewpoint that is a knowledge of Siberia. For those willing to endure a panorama of thousands of miles of passing birch, there are occasional glimpses of this foreboding, long-forbidden and fascinating other world — Siberian Russia.

Riding the Trans-Siberian

The *Rossiya* is the Trans-Siberian route's flagship train, offering some of the best accommodation, provided travellers book first class. This train features all sorts of novel technology previously unknown to Soviet railways, such as air-conditioning and fully operational, retention toilets. For the traveller solely looking to fill in the long line on their map between Moscow and the Pacific, this might be the best option. However, since *Rossiya* is largely reserved for through passengers, it isn't necessarily available for passengers looking to make stop-overs at intermediate destinations. For those looking to explore, there are a variety of other trains that ply different portions of the route. These often use older (or at least un-refurbished) traditional carriages. To better experience Siberia and break up the long journey, it is recommended that visitors consider at least one stop-over.

Among the complications of long-distance train travel in Russia (and elsewhere in the former Soviet Union) are the difficulty in procuring tickets and the necessity of reserving seats. Unlike in most European Union countries, Russian railways are not set up to accept travel passes that allow you the freedom simply to get on and off trains as you please. Such a concept remains completely foreign. Thus a journey, especially one with multiple stops, requires considerable planning and persistent navigating of the Russian bureaucracy necessary for ordering tickets, making hotel reservations and obtaining visas (best accomplished in that order). This can be intimidating, if not overwhelming. Unless the travellers are fluent in Russian and patient, the process is best accomplished with the aid of a tour operator or a native guide. There are a variety of agencies that will help prospective Trans-Siberian tourists plan their visit, and no shortage of detailed guidebooks specifically focused on the subject.

Travelling on secondary trains is not only less expensive, but also provides a variety of other benefits. On many traditional carriages it is still possible to open windows. While not especially desirable in the winter, an open window can allow for some fresh air in the warmer months and might be welcome on the later days of the Trans-Siberian experience, since most trains lack showers. It also makes photography much easier. Although once open, the windows can be difficult to close again.

One of the characteristics of the older stock is the coal-fired samovar at the ends of the carriages. These are enormous, rising nearly to the full height of the corridor, and are used to supply hot water for tea and, once-cooled, a clean source of drinking water. The older carriages feature a chimney for exhaust that extends through the roof so that, despite an electric locomotive leading the train, the aroma of coal smoke lends an historic sense to the trip.

One feature of Russian trains is the car attendant, usually a woman, known as a *provodnista*, who helps travellers on their journeys. Two attendants are assigned to each carriage and work in half-day shifts. They check you in on boarding the train, and ensure you are in the correct compartment and seat (there is no open/unreserved seating on long-distance trains). In addition they serve cups of tea and coffee (the first option is generally advised, despite normal preferences of one beverage over the other) and take out all the rubbish that seems to accumulate on long journeys.

Trains without retention toilets dump refuse onto the line. To avoid fouling stations and nearby communities *provodnistas* lock the toilets about 15 minutes before arriving at stations. They will pound on the door and vocally evict lingering passengers who have visited these facilities at inopportune times. As a result, it is advised to pay close attention to the timetable. Keep in mind that the railway operates on Moscow time throughout the journey, despite crossing 8 or 9 time zones.

Lake Baikal

Lake Baikal is one of the highlights of the Trans-Siberian route that can be experienced by travellers destined to Vladivostok, as well on both Trans-Manchurian and Trans-Mongolian routes. Situated in eastern Siberia south-east of Irkutsk in the Buryat Autonomous Republic, this is the world's largest freshwater lake and also the deepest. The average depth is 2,395 feet (730 m), with the deepest points more than a mile (1,609 m) below the surface. It is believed that the volume of water represents 80 per cent of all the fresh water in Russia. The lake has been estimated to be 20–25 million years old, and has been the site of human settlement since the Stone Age, with identifiable human activity dating back at least 15,000 years.

The lake is surrounded by mountains, which were a considerable impediment to the Trans-Siberian railway in its early years. Difficulties in engineering around the lake delayed completion. Between 1900 and 1904 trains were ferried across the lake between Port Baikal and Mysovaya on the eastern shore. An extension around the south-western portion of the lake was initially opened in 1904, although operational difficulties didn't completely do away with train ferries until 1916. The third major change to the Lake Baikal route occurred in 1950, when the Soviets dammed the Angara River, which flooded the valley below Irkutsk raising the level of the lake. Avoiding the dam and lower Angara valley required a completely new alignment built south from Irkutsk to reach a junction at Slyudyanka. This new line, among the most impressive parts of the Trans-Siberian journey, required some expensive engineering using reverse loops to maintain a steady gradient. The climb on the cut-off begins at the east end of the Irkursk

Above: A provodnista *cleans the name plate on the Moscow–Ulan Bator train. Heavy Russian passenger carriages are clean and functional, if not luxurious.*

Overleaf: Line relocations changed the path for through trains passing Lake Baikal, while the truncated portion of the 1904 Circumbaikal route, known as the Krugobaikalka, remains for excursion trains. This scenic line hugs the rock shelf along Baikal's rugged western shore.*

Above: Novosibirsk, 'New Siberia', is a city of nearly a million and a half people that owes its existence to the arrival of the Trans-Siberian railway and its bridging of the River Ob here. A long-distance train rolls across the modern bridge, which remains a key structure on the route.

Left: The Western Siberia Railway Museum near Novosibirsk displays a variety of historic railway equipment including this standard Soviet-era Class ER9, high-voltage, AC electric multiple unit train painted in a classic livery. Trains of this type were introduced in the early 1960s.

passenger station. Near the summit of the line the gradient reaches 2.3 per cent, the steepest on the entire route. The sinuous descent towards Lake Baikal offers some stunning views. East of Slyudyanka the line hugs the south-eastern shore with the mountains to the north visible beyond the far side of the lake.

A truncated, 53-mile (89-km) portion of the 1904 line, known as the Krugobaikalka, remains along the rugged western shore from Slyudyanka to Port Baikal for local service and excursions. This route features numerous tunnels as it skirts the lake on a rock shelf. It is one of the scenic diversions available for travellers who take the time to stay over and explore the Baikal region. For many visitors, Lake Baikal is the destination, as this immense inland sea offers outdoor water tourism. Ferries span the lake at various points, and a hydrofoil runs the length of it, while the northern reaches of the lake are accessible via the BAM route.

Above: This truncated portion of the 1904-built Circumbaikal route along Lake Baikal has been retained for local services. A steam excursion works the old trackage that until 1950 had served Trans-Siberian mainlines.

THE TRANS-MONGOLIAN ROUTE
Into the Lands of Ghengis Khan

BRIAN SOLOMON

A popular alternative to the Vladivostok route is the detour on the famous Trans-Mongolian line across the vast Mongolian plain and Gobi desert to China. This is a substantially newer railway line; construction began after the Second World War. By 1950, it had opened from the junction with the Trans-Siberian line at Zaudinski near the Soviet city of Ulan Ude, to reach southwards to the Mongolian capital at Ulan Bator (Ulaan Bataar). By 1955, the railway spanned Mongolia, running 690 miles (1,111 km) to reach the Chinese border at Erenhot (Erlian). Today, through Trans-Mongolian express passenger trains tend to be scheduled on a weekly basis, although there other long-distance trains as well.

Scenically located between the Khama Daban and Tsaga Daban ranges, the historic Russian city of Ulan Ude has been a trading centre since the 18th century.

It is among potential stop-over points for travellers on a variety of Trans-Siberian journeys. with sights such as a Russian Buddhist centre, a large locomotive works and an enormous sculpture of Lenin's head that seems entirely out of proportion with its surroundings. Here, trains heading to Mongolia uncouple their electric locomotives and change to diesel power, typically a Soviet-era 2M62.

South of Ulan Ude, the line follows the Selange River. Naushki is the Russian frontier point where travellers should anticipate a prolonged customs and immigration stop. Travellers are advised to secure visas for the Mongolian Peoples Republic in advance of travel. Expect another prolonged stop on the Mongolian side of the frontier at Sukhe Bator (Sukhbaator), where the Russian Railway's 2M62s are exchanged for similar models operated by the Mongolian Railway. Interestingly, Mongolia now uses American-designed, General Electric-built Evolution-series diesels on some of its heavy freights.

Once on the move, free from the rigours of Russian-Mongolian frontier bureaucracy, passenger trains amble diagonally across the eastern Mongolian steppe towards Ulan Bator. The railway is largely a single track line that curves and sweeps through a sublimely barren landscape. Scenery changes quickly once into Mongolia. This is the land of the infamous Asian, horse-riding, military

Above: A Mongolian Railway Soviet-built 2M62 diesel-electric locomotive leads a Trans-Mongolian passenger train at Ulan Bator. Mongolian railways were largely built to Russian parameters and until recently primarily used Soviet-built equipment. However, recent locomotive acquisitions include American-designed, General Electric Evolution-series diesels.

strategist and conqueror, Temujin, better known by his assumed name — Genghis Khan — whose empire once spanned the continent centred at Karakorum, an ancient city south-west of the present capital at Ulan Bator.

Today Ulan Bator is Mongolia's largest city, and although characterized by smog and Stalinist, concrete tower blocks, makes for a fascinating sojourn as well as a jumping-off point for further Mongolian exploration. The city is famously cold in winter, but the people tend to be welcoming to visitors. Sights include the Bogdkhan Palace, Choijin Lama monastery, and a museum of natural history full of stuffed animals and petrified dinosaur eggs. Since through trains tend to make a prolonged stop at Ulan Bator, travellers who don't plan to layover will find this provides a good place to stretch their legs and take a photo or two of the train.

Through travellers will delight in the Mongolian Railways' dining car added to their Moscow-Beijing consist. This offers a different variety of cuisine from its Russian counterpart, reputedly of higher quality as well.

South of Ulan Bator the railway continues its winding passage across the grassy steppes, then crosses the Gobi desert where long stretches of tangent (straight) track make for curious, if somewhat tedious progress. Watch out for the

Above: A Trans-Mongolian passenger train rolls through the Soviet-style suburbs of Ulan Bator. The city has approximately 1.3 million people in a nation of just under 3 million.

Opposite top: Across central Asia nomads live in portable circular tents known as yurts, a common variation is the Mongolia ger, seen here from a Trans-Mongolian train.

Opposite below: Beijing is the final railway destination for many Trans-Siberian/Trans-Mongolian travellers. This populous Chinese metropolis offers many sites of interest to explore.

characteristic abode of central Asian nomads, the circular low tent known as a yurt. These are used by families from Kazakhstan to Chinese Mongolia; the Mongolian variation is known as a ger.

Crossing into China requires more bureaucracy. Through trains also need to change bogies on the Chinese side of the frontier at Erenhot, where the Russian broad gauge wheel-sets are exchanged for those with four foot 8½ inch (1,435 mm) gauge (used by Chinese railways) for the remainder of the journey.

Beijing may be viewed as the end of the journey, or simply the layover for the next leg of the trip by rail. China is an intensively rail-connected nation that has recently made enormous investments in new high-speed lines. For serious travellers considering a round trip back to Moscow, there is the option of riding the Trans-Manchurian route back to the Trans-Siberian, or consider the famed Silk Road route via Kazakhstan.

These pages: Indian Railways diesel-hydraulic locomotive 705 leads the Toy Train to Shimla in 2012. The line to Shimla uses tracks just 2 feet 6 inches (762 mm) in width, placing it among the world's narrowest gauge lines hosting a regular diesel-hauled passenger service.

PAKISTAN
RAILS OVER THE KHYBER PASS
A Conceptual Journey from Karachi to Landi Kotal

BRIAN SOLOMON

The Khyber Pass is a narrow rocky cleft near the border between Pakistan and Afghanistan, believed to be one of the world's most strategic mountain passes. Being on the most direct trade route between India and Central Asia, this rocky defile has seen the passage of Alexander the Great's armies and many succeeding military expeditions. The descendants of Alexander's armies still reside in the tribal, barren lands to the west of the pass. British colonial ambitions were thwarted on several occasions by the Afghans in the 19th century,

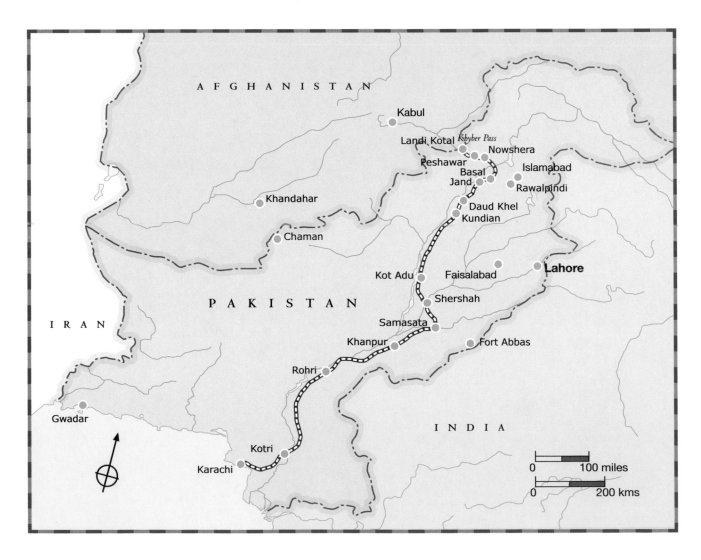

with the Khyber Pass being among the focal points of conflict. By the late 19th century, a strategic railway was being considered by the British. A false start in the early 20th century was abandoned before it got very far, and it wasn't until the advent of the so-called 'Third Afghan War', which followed in the wake of the First World War, that the Khyber Railway was finally built.

The elusive nature of this international friction point — a high mountain gateway for invading armies, combined with sublime barren beauty, outstanding engineering and an impossibly infrequent rail service, make the Khyber arguably the most exotic of any rail journey. However, a journey over the Khyber Railway isn't currently attainable owing to its difficult natural setting and hostile human environment. Even in recent times when the line wasn't washed out, the lands served by it were notoriously difficult to visit, and the service erratic.

Constructed in the long tradition of British railways by a Colonel Hearn in the 1920s, the line was formally opened to traffic on 3 November 1925. It connected Jamrud (near Peshawar), site of a military fort 1,469 feet (448 m) above sea level, and the similarly strategic citadel at Landi Kotal, 3,494 feet (1,065 m) ASL. Its precipitously steep extension down the west side of the pass to the Afghan frontier also opened 1925, but closed only seven years later. Deemed by M.B.K. Malik, author of *A Hundred Years of Pakistan Railways*, to be one of the great engineering achievements of its time, as built it included 92 bridges and culverts and

no fewer than 34 tunnels, plus two switchbacks on the east slope and another two on the short-lived west slope.

Make no mistake, this railroad was built for military strategic purposes, and the role it played in trade or tourism was secondary to its ability to move troops to the mouth of the Khyber. Even today, a look at Google Earth will reveal a sizeable railway yard at Landi Kotal, a location that even when scheduled trains were operated saw but one weekly passenger train in each direction. As late as 2008, it was possible to charter excursions to Landi Kotal, but now the line is in limbo.

Above: A train for Landi Kotal is seen at one of the line's famous switchbacks (an arrangement of stub-end tracks, sometimes called 'zigzags,' used to gain elevation where a through line is impractical). The switchback necessitated reverse moves and so trains to the Khyber Pass worked 'topped and tailed' with locomotives at each end.

The *Khyber Mail* and Others

Elsewhere in Pakistan, passenger trains operate on a regular basis. The run between Karachi and Peshawar is still made by the evocatively named *Khyber Mail*, a train once used by passengers continuing onwards to Landi Kotal. By and large, Pakistan's railways reflect British operating practice. Railway enthusiast, Michael Walsh, who some years ago visited Karachi on his way to the Khyber Pass, noted that this busy terminal was built in the British tradition, but with an exotic twist that reflected the atmosphere of the Indian subcontinent. "It was designed to keep people cool, and it was indeed hot outside." Signal boxes in the station used classic British-style mechanical lower quadrant signalling.

Michael was travelling with a tour group that had pre-booked tickets. "I was thus spared the ordeal of buying tickets, which seemed to involve fighting your way to the booking office." The railway men were very professional, and like railway men the world around, had an interest in their work. "I'd brought with me from Ireland some working timetables. I went into the railway office, and it was very much like you'd expect to find in England, with a British style of management. It was full of people, but I found some who were very open to trading my timetables for some of theirs. It wasn't often they had the opportunity to see how things were done in some other, to them, relatively exotic place."

Travelling on the mainline on a hot, dry and dusty September day, Michael found the railway impressive. "This was a well-engineered double track line. It seemed that track speed was good for about 70 mph (110 kph), and our train did just that. Especially distinctive were impressive bridges over the rivers, which all had armed watchmen or guards stationed in sentry boxes at each end."

Below: A mountain station on Pakistan Railways' route to the Khyber Pass. Built for its strategic military advantages, this route hosted a Sunday-only passenger train for many years. Now it is closed, a victim of washouts and political instability in the region. However, the tracks remain and perhaps someday it may reopen.

INDIA
TRAIN TO THE RAJ: KALKA TO SHIMLA
The Preserved Narrow Gauge Railway

PAUL BIGLAND

It may not be as famous as the 'toy train' to Darjeeling, but the Kalka to Shimla narrow gauge railway in the west Indian states of Haryana and Himachal Pradesh ranks as another of the world's great railway journeys. It's also included in the UNESCO World Heritage List as part of the World Heritage Site 'Mountain Railways of India'. The four-and-a-half hour trip to Shimla offers some breathtaking views whilst the journey is a memorable experience in itself.

By 1864 Shimla had become the summer capital of the British Raj and also the headquarters of the British army in India but communication with the outside world was via village cart. This situation led to the construction of a 59-mile (96-km)

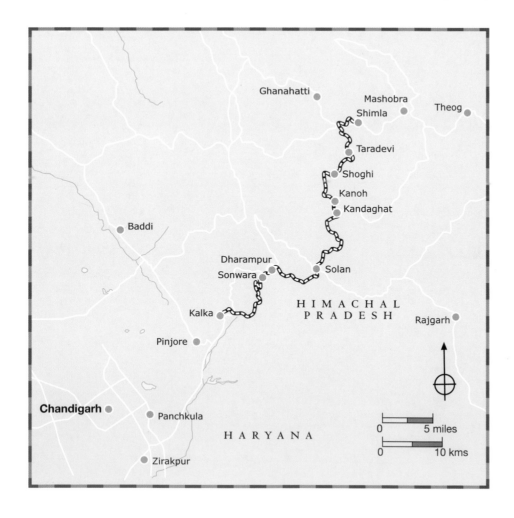

long narrow gauge railway that opened in 1898. Building the line was no easy matter. It involved the construction of 107 tunnels (although only 102 remain) plus 864 bridges and viaducts, some of which are substantial, such as the 'Arch Gallery', situated between Kandaghat and Kanoh stations. This is an arch bridge in three stages, constructed with stone masonry in the manner of an ancient Roman aqueduct. Another, Bridge No. 226, between Sonwara and Dharampur is an arch gallery bridge having five tier galleries of multiple spans, constructed from stone masonry and bridging a deep valley surrounded by high peaks.

Above: On the Kalka to Shimla narrow gauge railway, the scenery becomes dramatic and rugged between Solan and Shimla with stunning views as the line ascends steep valleys.

Spectacular scenery along the whole route and the marvels of its construction keep travellers on the line spellbound. The best views are to be found by sitting on the right of the train on the way up to Shimla and on the left on the way down. Regular trains consist of six little blue-and-cream coaches with wooden seats, hauled by powerful small diesel engines, although tourists can hire their own private luxury coach (the *Shivalik Queen*) to attach to the public train, or use the tiny *Himalayan Queen* railcar.

On leaving Kalka, 2,152 feet (656 m) above sea level, the railway meanders through sprawling suburbs, then enters the foothills and immediately commences its climb. The line loops back upon itself several times in the first few miles using the contours of the land to gain height as it passes through a series of rapidly expanding small towns. The most notable town on the route is Solan, which is considered to be a mini Shimla. A festival celebrating the goddess Shoolini Devi, after whom the city is named, is held each summer in June. More materially and perhaps more widely known is the Solan brewery (India's oldest) which was set up by a Briton, Edward Dyer, to brew the famous Lion beer.

Between Solan and Shimla the scenery becomes more rugged and the views more dramatic. Steep, terraced valleys dominate the landscape and the railway twists and turns like a snake, burrowing through tunnels or leaping across ravines on arches. Passengers get a chance to recover their breath (and enjoy a cup of tea) at small stations where the train pauses in passing loops before finally reaching lofty Shimla, which is perched atop a ridge at 4,600 feet (1,400 m) giving some wonderful views of the snow-capped Himalayas beyond.

JAPAN
HOKKAIDO'S LOCAL TRAINS
Japanese Contrasts

SCOTT LOTHES

okkaido, the northernmost of Japan's four main islands, boasts two of the fastest, diesel-powered, narrow gauge trains in the world: the *Super Hokuto* and *Super Ozora* limited express trains, which run the Sapporo-

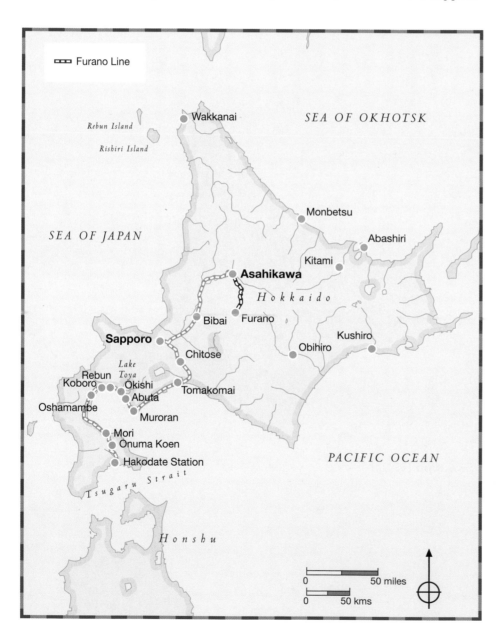

Furano Line

Rebun Island
Rishiri Island
Wakkanai
SEA OF OKHOTSK

Monbetsu

SEA OF JAPAN
Abashiri
Kitami
Asahikawa
Hokkaido
Bibai   Furano
Kushiro
Sapporo   Obihiro
Chitose
Lake Toya
Rebun
Koboro   Okishi
Abuta   Tomakomai
Oshamambe
Muroran
Mori
Onuma Koen
Hakodate Station
Tsugaru Strait
PACIFIC OCEAN

Honshu

0   50 miles
0   50 kms

Hakodate and Sapporo-Kushiro routes respectively, using tilting, multiple-unit trainsets with top speeds of 80 mph (130 kph). The average speeds of these trains are even more impressive when you consider the mountainous terrain, curving tracks and the number of stops they make.

The *Super Ozora* traverses the biggest mountain range on the island, covering 216½ miles (348 km) at an average speed of 54½ mph (87.8 kph), which includes four intermediate stops. The *Super Hokuto* hustles along the rugged Pacific Coast at an average clip of 56½ mph (91 kph) on its 198-mile (319-km) run, which includes no fewer than 11 station stops. With that kind of performance and frequent service on both lines, these trains compete very effectively with domestic flights. But if you really want to see Hokkaido by train, you shouldn't take either one of them.

For a more intimate experience of Hokkaido by rail, get on board a local train. They are not difficult to find. Almost every stretch of railway on the island has local passenger service, typically several times daily. The trains usually comprise

Above: KiHa 40 bringing up the rear of a three-car local train stopping at remote Koboro Station, located between two long tunnels, on the Muroran Main Line.

one or two boxy, self-propelled diesel railcars. They lack the sleek looks and tilting mechanisms of the expresses, but most of them can still hit 60 or 70 mph (95 or 115 kph) — although they rarely get the chance. Stations are spaced every few miles, even out in the countryside, and most local trains stop at every station along their routes. Your journey will assuredly take longer by local train, but you will just as assuredly see more along the way.

While the express trains whisk dark-suited 'salarymen' from one meeting to another, the local trains cater to a more convivial clientele. Riding local trains, you are more likely to find grandmothers on shopping trips and students going to and from school. Except for kindergarten, there are no school buses in Japan, so middle and high school students regularly commute by train. You are likely to overhear groups of them practising English in hushed voices. If you are lucky, before they get to their stop, the bravest in the group just might work up enough nerve to strike up a conversation with you.

The best times of year to take long trips by local trains are around the school holidays, when the *Seishun juhachi kippu* — youthful eighteen ticket — is available. Despite its name, people of any age can buy this pass, and for about US$100, you get five days of unlimited travel on local trains anywhere in the country. You are still likely to ride with students, as they will often be taking vacation trips of their own. There are three school holiday periods yearly: March through early April, late July to early September and early December to early January. With Hokkaido's mild summers, you can take advantage of another perk of local train travel during the warmer months — windows that actually open.

The same 198-mile (319-km) trip from Sapporo to Hakodate that takes three-and-a-half hours by express takes more than twice that by local train, and you will have to change trains three times. Not all of the connections are tight, so if you find yourself with time to kill in some unknown place like Oshamambe, take advantage of the opportunity. Leave the station, stroll the streets, find a noodle shop and ponder the changes that time has wrought on rural Hokkaido.

Hokkaido is the most recent major addition to Japan, fully colonized in the mid-1800s for its abundant natural resources. Its native people, the Ainu of Mongolian descent, were assimilated and eradicated with much of the same brutal efficiency as was carried out on American Indians. Few traces of Ainu culture remain. To find them, leave your train at Shiraoi and walk half a mile (800 m) east from the station, on the north side of the tracks, to the Shiraoi Ainu Museum, arguably the best museum about the Ainu people in all of Japan.

Coal, timber and seafood brought the Japanese to Hokkaido, and coal, in particular, led to rapid industrialization. The trip between Sapporo and Hakodate takes you over a portion of one of the island's first railways, built from interior

Opposite: A pair of KiHa 40 diesel multiple units climbs Joumon Pass on the Sekihoku Main Line in central Hokkaido on a bright morning.

coalmines to the fabulous natural harbour of Muroran. To fully explore that harbour, leave the main line at Higashi-Muroran and take a four-mile (6.5-km) jaunt on the branch line along the Etomo Peninsula to Muroran proper. The ride will take you past steel mills struggling for life in a largely post-industrial economy and leave you wondering how this city that looks to have come straight from the American Rust Belt wound up on the Japanese coast.

Muroran's mills and Hokkaido's coalmines boomed through the first two-thirds of the 20th century, but then Japanese economic and energy policies changed. Cheaper coal began to be imported from China and Australia, and Hokkaido's mines fell silent. Muroran's population has plummeted from 160,000 in the 1960s to barely 90,000 today. Interior mining hubs like Yubari suffered far greater declines. Today Hokkaido's capital of Sapporo is one of the fastest-growing cities in Japan, but on the whole, the island's population is shrinking. With fewer jobs in the countryside, rural Hokkaidians are either moving to Sapporo or leaving the island altogether. The express trains move fast enough that you may not notice these changes, but if you ride the local trains, you can spot the signs everywhere.

Below: A single KiHa 150 rolls through rice paddies along the Muroran Main Line near Abuta on a hazy afternoon. Volcano Bay is in the background.

South-west of Muroran, heading towards Hakodate, the scenery opens up and soon becomes quite dramatic. Abuta (Toya Station) is the gateway to Lake Toya, part of the Shikotsu-Toya National Park reached by a direct bus service from the Toya Station. Beyond Abuta, the railway plays hide-and-seek with the bay, punching through a series of tunnels and clinging to a narrow, rocky shelf right beside the water. Winter sunsets can be fabulous in the late afternoons, while seaside camping is available in the warmer months near the Rebun and Okishi stations, which are served only by local trains.

To get about as far from civilization as you can go by train in Japan, disembark at Koboro Station, an unlikely stop right between two long tunnels. Originally built as a signal station, Koboro became an unofficial stop for local trains of the Japanese National Railways. When Japan privatized its railways in 1987, Koboro was 'grandfathered in' as an official station. One Japanese railway website rates it as the number one *hikyoh eki* (remote station) in the entire country. A trail leads down to a scenic, deserted beach in a small cove, while another trail leads to a larger cove that includes a Shinto shrine built into a cave. Check carefully, as only half of the local trains stop at Koboro.

Above: A three-car 711-series electric local train passing the mills of the Japan Steel Works in Muroran.

Further south, Onuma Koen station provides access to Onuma Quasi National-al Park, which includes two lakes, miles of trails and the volcano, Mt Komagatake.

Hakodate is charming seaport on Hokkaido's southern coast, with an extensive streetcar system, exquisite seafood and one of the best night views on the island. Mt Hakodate looks down on the heart of the city, built on the narrow isthmus between Hakodate Bay and the Tsugaru Strait. The strait connects the Pacific Ocean to the Sea of Japan and separates Hokkaido from Honshu, largest island of the Japanese archipelago. Ferries still ply the strait, but since 1988, the 33½-mile (54-km) long Seikan Tunnel under the strait has connected Hokkaido to the rest of the Japanese railway network. Local trains do not operate through the tunnel, but local train tickets are honoured on express trains between the last station on either side of the tunnel.

Travelling by local train also gives you a second routing option for the northern half of the trip between Sapporo and Hakodate. Instead of the Muroran Line, which is also used by all of the express and freight trains, you can change trains in Oshamambe and take the original Hakodate Line. The Hakodate Line was the first railway to connect Sapporo to Hakodate, and it is still shorter but much steeper than the coast-hugging Muroran Line. Today only local trains ply the mountainous portion of the Hakodate Line between Oshamambe and Otaru, a suburb west of Sapporo. The mountains boast some of the best skiing in Japan — the slopes of Niseko are world-renowned and dictate special winter ski trains from Sapporo. There are also breathtaking views of Mt Yotei, the 'Fuji of Hokkaido', and the Sea of Japan.

Getting from Sapporo to Kushiro entirely by local train will take even longer than either of the Hakodate options. In 1981, the new Sekisho Line opened to the east of Sapporo, creating a more direct route to Kushiro via a remarkably-well engineered mountain railway replete with long tunnels, fills and viaducts. Only freights and expresses run the length of the Sekisho Line, though. The only way to get from Sapporo to Kushiro entirely by local train is to take the original railway route, which leaves Sapporo to the north-east up the broad Ishikari River valley on the Hakodate Line towards Asahikawa. Change trains in Takikawa on the Nemuro Line, which runs via Furano, another renowned winter ski destination. After additional train changes in Furano and Obihiro, you will finally arrive in Kushiro a little more than ten hours after departing Sapporo — two-and-a-half times longer than the trip takes by express.

Travelling by local train is about more than just covering miles, though. The slower trains offer the flexibility to stop and explore at any station along the line, and well-timed bus connections, even at rural stations, often expand the traveller's reach. Consider a side trip from Furano up the scenic Furano Line to

Asahikawa, where you will find rolling fields of lavender in the early summer beneath a backdrop of snow-capped peaks — the aptly-named Daisetsuzan or literally 'Big Snow Mountains' that are Hokkaido's backbone. Daisetsuzan National Park, the largest in Japan, includes 16 peaks in excess of 6,560 feet (2,000 m) and miles upon miles of hiking and backpacking trails.

You can, in fact, go almost everywhere in Hokkaido by local train, and every corner of the island is reachable from Sapporo in a single day. If you make it to

Above: With 6,227-foot (1,898-m) Mt Yotei standing tall in the distance, a local train with two KiHa 150 DMUs cruises along the Shiribetsu River on the Hakodate Main Line near Niseko.

Above: *KiHa 54 on the Senmo Line crossing the Shari River in Shari, Hokkaido, near the Shiretoko Peninsula. The 5,075-foot (1,547-m) Mt Shari looms in the background.*

Left: *A one-car morning local train with a KiHa 40 bound for Furano climbs the Karikachi Pass on the Sekisho Line near Shintoku.*

Kushiro, consider heading north up the Senmo Line through the wetlands of Kushiro-shitsugen National Park and onto Shiretoko National Park on the island's narrow, north-eastern peninsula. You can also ride all the way up the Soya Line to Wakkannai, the northernmost train station in Japan, where you can catch ferries to the remote and scenic islands of Rishiri and Rebun and maybe even catch a glimpse of the Russian island of Sakhalin. Wherever you go by local train in Hokkaido, or anywhere in Japan, you are sure to find adventure and a deeper understanding of the land and its people — and of their connections to Japan's railways. The Japanese continue to grow up with trains — and especially their local trains. They ride them to school and to work, on business trips and for family vacations. Thanks in large part to the local trains of Japan, the railroad there is still a common thread in the fabric of everyday life.

Above: Two-car northbound local train with a KiHa 150 leading a KiHa 40 running along Volcano Bay on the Muroran Main Line at Toyoura late in the afternoon with fiery fall foliage.

SRI LANKA
COLOMBO TO KANDY AND ONWARDS INTO THE HILLS
An Asian Delight

PAUL BIGLAND

In these uncertain times it is a delight to find a country that is shrugging off the effects of a civil war, re-opening long-closed railway lines and providing the opportunity to explore a vibrant and colourful landscape.

Trains are comfortable, with three classes: third class is dirt-cheap but the wooden benches are always crowded; second class has padded seats and fans and is less crowded; first class has air-conditioned coaches, observation saloons and sleeping berths. One idiosyncrasy of Sri Lankan railways is that most coaches have

seats labelled 'reserved for clergy', so if you think you can pass for a Buddhist monk you should have no trouble! Otherwise, reservations can be made on most, but not all, trains and fares are remarkably cheap. But don't expect the trains to run on time – speed is not of the essence here, which is part of the attraction. Buffet cars are supplied on the main expresses, but these are not for the fastidious.

Left: Sri Lankan class M6 diesel-electric 792 approaches the station at Haputale with a long passenger train. Classic British-style semaphores govern train movements on the line.

Below: The Podi Menike (which translates as 'Little Maiden') ascends the hill country amidst tropical scenery and a relaxed operational atmosphere.

My last trip encompassed a journey from the southern town of Matara (an area with some superb beaches) to the hill station of Kandy and beyond towards Badulla.

Our start, Matara, the southern terminus of the line 100 miles (160 km) from Colombo is a typical one-platform station. In between the arrival of the trains, an air of torpor descends on the place, with goats using the canopies as shelter from the sun. The only sign of life is from the refreshment room, which supplies excellent, spicy *rotis* (stuffed bread). As it wasn't possible to reserve seats for the Colombo train we simply turned up 30 minutes early and sat in the empty stock in the sidings – common practice here! The line from Matara hugs the coast to Galle passing palm-fringed beaches, lagoons and small villages on its way. At Colombo we changed trains for Kandy heading inland past rice paddies on either side of the track to Polgahawela Junction, where the lines to the north of the country diverge and the climb to Kandy begins.

From here the scenery changes, the rice paddies are left behind as the countryside becomes hilly and the line returns to single track. A rising gradient of 1 in 44 dominates the climb to Kadugannawa, which is 1,700 feet (520 m) above sea level, a height appreciated from Balan, where at Sensation Rock a sheer precipice of 1,000 feet (300 m) is just outside your window. The views (coupled with the drop) are truly breathtaking! After this, the last stretch of the 74-mile (120-km) journey into Kandy seems anti-climactic.

Above: The Podi Menike passes Kotagala plantations on its leisurely journeys.

Opposite: Locomotive 784 ambles over the line at Ella, Sri Lanka. This is one of 16 M6 class diesel-electrics built by German manufacturer Thyssen-Henschel.

THE *UDARATA MENIKE*

BERNARD VAN CUYLENBURG

The train from Colombo to Badulla was originally hauled by two steam engines. This was replaced by the *Udarata Menike*, introduced in 1954 and powered by two British diesel locomotives. A new set of carriages was hitched onto the diesel locomotives on her maiden run, and that's how it remained. The icing on the cake was the presentation of twelve Canadian diesel locomotives under the Colombo Plan in the late 1950s — an outright gift from the Canadian government under the premiership of Pierre Trudeau. These diesels were a joy to behold, and I still remember the names of some of them, on either side of the locomotive gleaming in silver and blue. They were *Alberta*, *Montreal*, *Saskatchewan*, *Prince Edward Island*, *Vancouver*, *Manitoba*, *Toronto* and *Ontario*. Out went the British locomotives — at least on the up-country run – and in came one Canadian diesel to take their place. I later picked up some trivia about the Canadian locomotives. The distances they covered in Canada sometimes ran to over a thousand miles, apparently the distance from Colombo to Badulla was insufficient for these 2,500 horse-power diesels, so after the *Menike* reached Badulla around 6.20 p.m. each evening, the locomotive had to be kept running for some hours, even though the journey had ended! Apparently, one locomotive could provide electricity for an entire town.

During my last visit to Sri Lanka in 2000, I was pleased to see some of the Canadian locomotives still riding the rails. On a trip from Haputale to Colombo in the *Udarata Menike* we crossed the *Podi Menike*, the younger sister of the *Udarata Menike*, which I observed was hauled by a Canadian diesel locomotive, *Montreal*. The *Udarata Menike* — 'The Maid of the Mountains' or, as I prefer to call her 'The Maid of the Mists' – will forever travel the corners of our minds in the realms of memory on a journey that has no end.

SOUTHEAST ASIA
VIETNAM'S *REUNIFICATION EXPRESS*
Hanoi to Ho Chi Minh City

SCOTT LOTHES

Through low clouds clinging to the rugged mountains above the South China Sea, I rode enthralled at an open window of a Vietnam Railways passenger train. As the two-tone blue express twisted slowly through the coastal forests, a man emerged from the trees and began running in step with the locomotive. Suddenly, he reached up, grabbed a handrail and swung himself onto the side of the train. My pulse quickened as the combined horrors of an Old West hold-up and a modern-day terrorist attack flashed through my mind. Yet my fellow window travellers, natives of the land, showed not the slightest signs of concern.

I had boarded the train the previous morning in Ho Chi Minh City (formerly Saigon), Vietnam's largest metropolis. The 1,072-mile (1,725-km) rail line running north to the capital city of Hanoi is a great source of national pride, symbolic of the country's reunification in 1976 following decades of war. The railway was completed in 1936 during French colonial rule and remained intact for only 18 years, cut politically by the 1954 Geneva Accords and subsequently ravaged by floods, and bombing and other forms of sabotage.

So strategic is the route that when North and South Vietnam merged, the new government gave top priority to rebuilding the railway. The 'biggest project' of the reunified nation's first year required 70,000 people to repair or reconstruct 200 bridges, 500 culverts, 20 tunnels and 150 stations. When the first train from Ho Chi Minh City arrived in Hanoi on January 4, 1977, the Associated Press reported it "was greeted by thousands of persons waving flags and setting off firecrackers".

My present concern of something considerably stronger than firecrackers was, of course, wholly unfounded. The man hanging off the side of the train climbed a ladder and sat down on the roof. A few minutes later, he climbed back down as we approached a cottage at the edge of the forest. He jumped off and jogged onto the porch, where he joined his family around the breakfast table, turning back and waving with a big grin.

The trains between Ho Chi Minh City and Hanoi have been dubbed the *Reunification Express* to commemorate how the railway has helped bring the country together. Service is frequent, with at least five daily departures from either end of the line (more during busy travel times like the Tet holidays), but it is not fast

Above: A station attendant at Ho Chi Minh City.

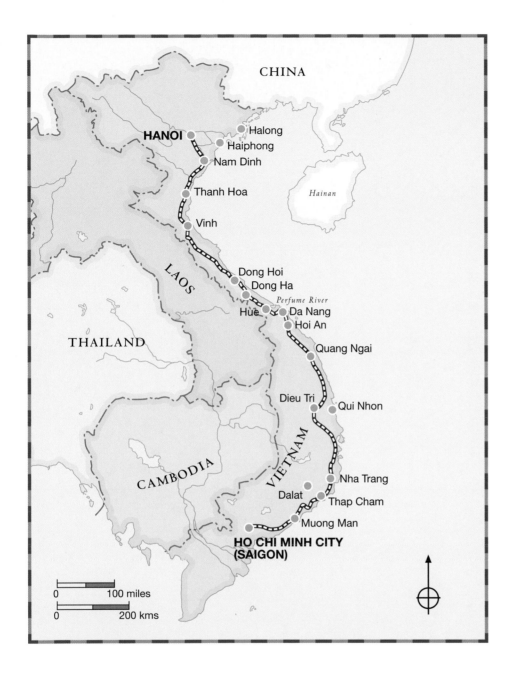

– the quickest schedule averages barely more than 30 mph (48 kph) – but speed is not the point.

The trundling trains offer intimate looks into both the land and the people of Vietnam. In large cities, the tracks frequently run right next to shops and apartments. In Hanoi, street vendors set up shop right on the main line, which is tightly flanked by buildings on both sides. They quickly move their tables whenever a slow-moving train approaches and just as quickly re-establish themselves once the train has passed. Crowds often greeted our train during station stops at smaller cities, where food sellers did brisk business from the platforms.

Above: Northbound train SE6 seen approaching Hue.

Left: Northbound passenger train SE6 meeting a southbound freight train near the summit of Hai Van Pass.

Freight trains share the metre-gauge tracks, and freight operations often take place right next to the passenger platforms. At one small-city station, a group of several workers used a small crane to load logs into open-top freight cars. Our northbound express, train SE6, passed several freight trains waiting in sidings. The freights were typically about 20 cars long and pulled by a single four-axle diesel locomotive. Romanian-built model D11H (1,100 hp) and Czech-built model D12E (1,200 hp) locomotives predominated in freight service, as well as on the more basic passenger trains. In both cases, a second locomotive was added to the rear of these trains for the steep grades of Hai Van Pass between Da Nang and Hue. Newer, more powerful, six-axle D19E locomotives from China (1,950 hp) handle the express passenger trains and tackle the mountain grades without the assistance of a helper locomotive.

While we did see some other international travellers on board train SE6, we were surrounded by Vietnamese. The station in Ho Chi Minh City was crowded with families carrying luggage, shopping bags and cardboard boxes containing everything from clothing to food to electronics. We played Uno with a group of curious children, talked long into the night with an English-speaking woman in our sleeping-car compartment and even when we shared no common language with our fellow passengers, we still found other ways to communicate.

Above: A D19E locomotive with a southbound passenger train descends the Hai Van Pass near Da Nang.

Just getting to the train station in Ho Chi Minh City had required some creative communication. The taxi driver had not understood any English terms for 'railway station', so I had to resort to pantomime to get my point across. This had come as something of a surprise after two days in Ho Chi Minh City, where seemingly every person employed in the tourist trade knew all of the English terms necessary to do his or her job. But then again, just getting the train tickets had taken unexpected effort and persistence in the face of local travel agents pushing cheap domestic flights and special tourist buses.

Most of the passenger trains on Vietnam's north-south main line make the entire run between the country's two largest cities. We took ours as far as Hue, centre of traditional culture and the first stop north of Hai Van Pass. Immediately north of the station, the railway crosses the Perfume River on a long, through-truss bridge. The river flows out of low, rolling hills to the west in which the colonial emperors are entombed. The next day we hired a 'dragon boat' for a leisurely cruise under the railway bridge and up the river to visit the tombs.

Further to the north of Hue, the railway passes through the demilitarized zone (DMZ), where monuments commemorate what is known in Vietnam as 'The American War'. Seen from the windows of a *Reunification Express* train, the DMZ today is a quiet, agricultural land where the rice grows blindingly green, cone-hatted villagers ride rusty bicycles on the roadsides and cows calmly munch the

Above: A southbound freight train crossing the Perfume River and passing a dragon boat at Hue.

weeds growing out of four-decade-old bomb craters. Half a mile (800 m) south of the former border, we watched children pouring out of a yellow, one-story elementary school to go home for lunch. Small groups of them stopped and waved excitedly as we passed. During our entire time in Vietnam, we never witnessed the slightest hint of animosity towards Americans.

It was sometimes hard to realize that a war was ever fought in Vietnam, although the reminders are literally around every corner. What was not hard to realize was the connection between the people and their land. I've seen that same connection in the eyes of nearly everyone I've ever met who has worked hard to live on the land. It seems so clear now, how similar we all are. I wonder how it could have looked any different, 50 years ago.

From Hoi An I caught another northbound train and continued to Hanoi, arriving just before sunrise to find the station buzzing with activity. Not long after our train arrived from the south, three other passenger trains were scheduled to depart, bound for three different destinations on three different branch lines to the north, near the Chinese border.

For the last night of the trip, I slept aboard a boat in Halong Bay. The bay is a World Heritage Site, and in local legend it was formed by dragons that came from the heavens to protect Vietnam from foreign invaders. Leaning on the third-deck railing as the seemingly-endless karst formations slipped past our gliding boat, I spotted fishing villages in remote coves and my mind drifted freely to musings about the lives of these fishing families.

So much of Vietnam is so accessible, so easy to see thanks to English-speaking staff, affordable prices (at least for western visitors) and friendly locals eager for foreign tourist dollars. Yet that same accessibility can keep the essence of the country just beyond reach. It's often in clear view, just beyond a barrier of window glass or boat railing. You can still experience it, although it takes some extra effort and a little courage, like boarding the Saigon River ferry, renting a bike for a country ride or insisting on those train tickets when seemingly every travel agent in the country wants you to try a different mode of conveyance.

Change is fast afoot in Vietnam, and while more modern conveniences and higher English literacy make the country easier to visit, they also make the essence of traditional life that much harder to experience. A new highway tunnel opened in 2005, bypassing the original road over Hai Van Pass — a spectacular route that today hosts only locals and intrepid tourists. Similar projects have been considered for the railway, with hopes to someday construct a new, high-speed line all the way from Ho Chi Minh City to Hanoi. If that happens, the man I presumed to be a train hijacker will have no choice but to walk back to his cottage in the forest on Hai Van Pass. For my part, I will always be glad for the time we shared a ride.

Above: A Vietnamese-built class D8E locomotive leads a northbound passenger train through the streets of Hanoi.

THE DALAT CRÉMAILLÈRE RAILWAY
Escape to a Vietnamese hill station

DAVID BOWDEN

Vietnam Railways operate 1,616 miles (2,600 km) of railway but no longer the branch line from the main north-south railway to the highlands of Dalat. The Crémaillère Railway (which is French for cog or rack and pinion) once linked Thap Cham on the coast near Phan Rang with the French hill station of Dalat in the Central Highlands. Hill stations developed throughout Asia as they offered cooler respite for heat-weary colonialists. Dalat's cool climate, lakes and forests ensure that it is still one of Vietnam's most tranquil holiday retreats. While hill tribe people or *montagnards* lived here for centuries, Dalat came to the attention of the French colonialists in 1893 when Dr Alexandre Yersin, a protégé of Louis Pasteur and the first to identify the plague bacillus, identified the area as a healthy retreat.

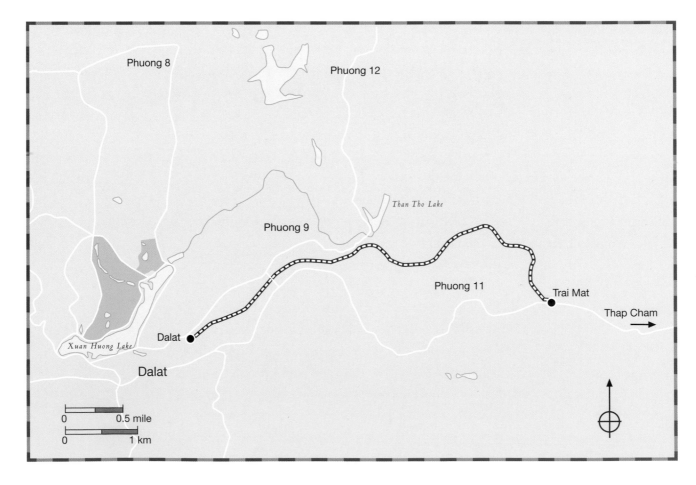

Sections of the 52-mile (84-km) long railway opened in 1928 but by 1964, the Viet Cong had successfully blown up enough of the line to force its closure. Initially surveyed in 1898 by the French, the fully completed line didn't open until 1933 due to steep sections near the summit of the highlands at 4,921 feet (1,500 m) above sea level. Some 10 miles (16 km) of the track had to incorporate zigzag sections and cog-wheel technology designed by Swedish engineers. When it opened, there were two daily train serves from coastal Nha Trang to Dalat and back, which included three passenger and one goods carriages. The operator was called the Compagnie des Chemins de Fer de L'Indochine and used locomotives built in Winterhur, Switzerland, and Germany.

Today, the only section of the line that is open is five miles (eight kilometres) long on the plateau from Dalat Station to the village of Trai Mat. There are currently five departures a day between the hours of 7.45 a.m. to 4 p.m. for the 30-minute round-trip through market gardens to the village of Trai Mat where the small Linh Phuoc Pagoda is the main attraction. Dalat's Art Deco station is worth visiting to admire the large clock, colonial ambiance and old locomotives on display, including a Japanese locomotive which was the last commercial steam train to operate in Vietnam. On the journey, passengers sit in restored carriages of the Dalat Plateau Rail Road and are hauled by a D6H locomotive. Who knows: one day the old Crémaillère Railway may be reinstated?

Above: Pine trees flourish around Dalat in the cool, forested mountains of the southernmost extremity of Central Vietnam.

Opposite: The old clock is a central feature of the façade of Dalat railway station.

SINGAPORE TO BANGKOK ON THE
EASTERN & ORIENTAL EXPRESS
Reliving a Golden Era

DAVID BOWDEN

Steam trains were introduced into Malaya (now Malaysia) in 1885 and by 1931 the west coast of peninsular Malaysia was connected by rail from the island of Singapore in the south to Padang Besar in the north on the border with Thailand. Grand hotels such as Raffles (Singapore), the Hotel Majestic (Kuala Lumpur) and the Eastern & Oriental (Penang) provided stylish accommodation then and still do today.

While public trains operated by Malaysia's Keratapi Tanah Melayu (KTM) use this line, the luxurious *Eastern & Oriental Express* has introduced a degree of panache recalling classic rail journeys of yesteryear but with contemporary creature comforts. It operates a few journeys each month from Singapore via Malaysia to Bangkok and vice versa. The *Eastern & Oriental Express* is one of the world's great train journeys and on the 'essential' list for many avid train travellers.

Below: The Eastern & Oriental Express crosses the famous Bridge over the River Kwai in Kanchanaburi where the passengers are able to explore the district's historic landmarks.

In the early colonial days, the train was the principal mode of transportation from Singapore northwards along the peninsula. While planes now make this journey at breakneck speed, there are some who seek comfort in the 'olden days', slipping back into the nostalgia of colonial Malaya.

Well-heeled passengers gather at Singapore's Raffles Hotel on the first morning of the journey. Trains once commenced the journey northwards in central Singapore but the terminus has been relocated to the Woodlands Immigration Centre in Singapore's far north. Passengers now travel by coach from their luxurious central Singapore hotels to Woodlands.

Above: Cream and racing green colours dominate the train from the logo to the glistening exterior. The logo features the Malayan Tiger, which was once common along the route but now is highly endangered.

The glistening, British racing green-and-cream livery of the 18-car *Eastern & Oriental Express* train awaits while staff deal with the immigration formalities before the train inches across the Johor Strait causeway into Malaysia and the recently-built Johor Bahru Station, where entry formalities into Malaysia are briskly completed.

Lunch and then afternoon tea are served in one of the train's three dining cars and in passenger cabins respectively. Meals that would be the envy of any high-calibre restaurant located on terra firma are served during the three-day, two-night journey. The hard-working culinary team creates gastronomic experiences at every sitting with dishes, such as tom yam vichyssoise with quail medallion and vegetable tagliatelle, pan-roasted sea bass served on a bed of Sichuan-styled vegetables and coconut ice cream with gula Melaka sago on the menu. Vintage wines are available by the bottle or glass. The dress code is smart casual during the day but in the evening, guests are expected to 'dress to kill' although not in the Agatha Christie *Murder on the Orient Express* sense.

Above: Passengers are served gourmet meals accompanied by vintage wines in the atmospheric surroundings of the two restaurant cars.

Pullman cabins are smartly decorated and efficient in their use of the limited space available. Compared to the KTM train which also plies the tracks, the cabins are spacious and include the luxury of toilet, shower, worktable and comfortable bed. Parquetry woodwork lines the walls and two-tone grey carpet provides a spring under foot. There are two berths in each cabin and the upper bunk is pushed to the wall during the day with the bottom bunk serving as a two-seat couch. Exclusive toiletries are provided as are an abundance of plush towels. Brass fittings, air-conditioning, antique lights and a decorative table provide a historic setting. Passengers are requested to restrict their cabin luggage to just one piece with any additional baggage stored in the luggage carriage.

The *Eastern & Oriental Express* is really about the journey as much as the destination. For many passengers, it doesn't seem to matter too much where they are heading as their immediate surroundings and the experience are paramount. The train only makes three scheduled stops on its journey – Kuala Lumpur, Butterworth (Penang) and Kanchanaburi (River Kwai, Thailand).

Kuala Lumpur is a brief evening stop with just sufficient time to appreciate arguably one of the world's finest railway stations. Built in the British Raj

Left: Lavish sleeping compartments featuring marquetry-lined walls are fitted with a sofa, which is folded down each evening to make a comfortable bed.

Below: The Bar Car is a popular place to relax and enjoy an exotic cocktail or a glass of fine wine available from a comprehensive menu.

architectural style, this delightfully ornate building was completed in 1911 according to British Railway specifications including the incorporation of a solid roof able to withstand several feet of snow; surely a highly improbable climatic event in the tropics. On departing the Kuala Lumpur city limits, a sumptuous dinner is served.

Passengers wake on day two in Butterworth and are then bussed across one of two bridges over the Straits of Malacca into Georgetown's bustling UNESCO World Heritage Site on the island of Penang. A trishaw ride around the heritage city is a highlight for most. Back on board, in the late afternoon, the train passes through rubber plantations and into Thailand with the open-air observation car and adjoining bar, the preferred locations for admiring the countryside. In his 1975 book *The Great Railway Bazaar*, Paul Theroux observed: 'and more frequently rubber estates intruded on jungle, a symmetry of scored trunks and trodden paths hemmed in by classic jungle, hanging lianas, palms like fountains, and a smothering undergrowth of noisy greenery all dripping in the rain'. Little has changed in the intervening years in northern Malaysia and southern Thailand. The train passes between the countries with seamless immigration and customs formalities.

On the morning of the third day the train has already passed through much of the isthmus of Thailand and rattles through rice fields towards Hong Pladuk Junction while passengers enjoy breakfast in bed. In some parts the track is so close to these people's houses it's as if the train passes through their backyards.

Above: Passengers can experience the countryside through which the train passes from the open-sided observation car positioned at the rear of the train.

The train continues down a spur line to Kanchanaburi with the whistle in overdrive to warn those traversing the numerous unmarked crossings. Kanchanaburi on the River Kwai has a special place in the hearts and minds of many whose relatives died in the construction of the infamous 'Death Railway' built for the Japanese during the Second World War. Tens of thousands of European and Asian forced labourers died in the railway's construction, making a visit to the Allied War Cemetery a very sombre experience.

By mid-afternoon on day three, the train pulls into Bangkok's Hua Lampong Station. Here the train is readied for its return journey with those travelling south from Bangkok taking four days and three nights to complete the journey. There are also the 'Ancient Kingdom of Lanna' journeys which head north from Bangkok, stopping on the way in Lampang and terminating at the former ancient Thai capital, Chiang Mai. A 'Fables of the Peninsula' journey taking in Kuala Lumpur, the Cameron Highlands, Penang and Huay Yan (south of Hua Hin, Thailand) has been recently introduced.

TRAINS FOR THE PEOPLE

While the well-to-do are wining and dining their way north or south, the public trains of Malaysia and Thailand operate along the same line using different rolling stock to provide a cheaper yet still exhilarating experience for overland travellers. Various classes are available from sit-up to sleepers with the second-class sleepers being seats that convert to up-down sleeping in the evening. The Thai trains provide reasonably sophisticated meals and beverages while the Malaysian trains have dining cars that mostly serve snacks.

Double tracking and electrification of the train line between Kuala Lumpur and Ipoh has enabled trains to travel at speeds of 93 mph (150 kph) on sections of the journey. This is being extended all the way to the Thai border and will ultimately provide a faster and more comprehensive service for travellers. The distance from Singapore to Bangkok is 1,233 miles (1,984 km) and the journey takes approximately 48 hours if there are no delays. The connections between trains in Kuala Lumpur, Butterworth and Hat Yai are not seamless and, in some cases, involve delays of several hours. There is an East Coast line in Malaysia that extends from the main north-south line at Gemas to terminate at Tumpat near Kota Bharu in the north-eastern state of Kelantan. Thailand is well serviced by trains and which provide an excellent way of discovering the country.

Above: *Modern express trains operate on the electrified railway line between Ipoh Station (pictured) and Kuala Lumpur.*

NORTH BORNEO'S RECREATED STEAM RAILWAY
A Jungle Train

DAVID BOWDEN

The loud shrill of the train whistle rings out across Tanjung Aru as the blackened steam locomotive slowly pulls out of the station on its exhilarating journey along Sabah's west coast to Papar some 44 miles (70 km) to the south of the state capital, Kota Kinabalu, on the island of Borneo.

Borneo comprises Sabah and Sarawak (two Malaysian states), the Sultanate of Brunei and Indonesian Kalimantan. The railway line from Tanjung Aru inland to the small town of Tenom has been the only railway line on the island

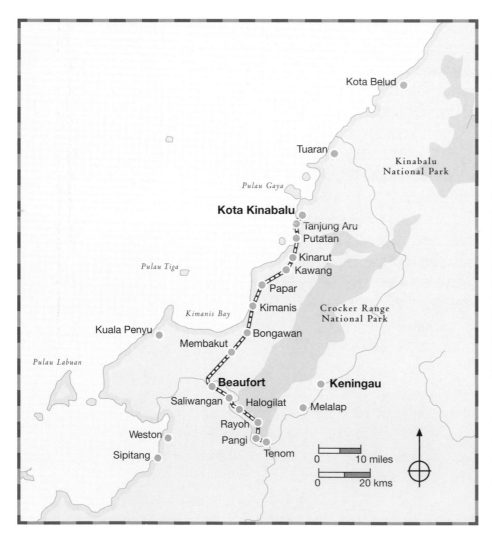

Above: The carriages of the North Borneo Railway are hauled by a Vulcan steam locomotive dating back to 1896 that is fuelled by firewood.

up until recently when a private freight line opened in Indonesian Kalimantan to facilitate the export of coal. The Sabah line was started in 1896 and remains as the only commercial railway on the world's third largest island.

Here, two trains operate – the public train owned by Sabah State Railway, which travels the entire distance to Tenom (see page 73) and the privately-owned North Borneo Railway (NBR), which has two tourist steam train journeys per week on Wednesdays and Saturdays. The former is an exciting journey to the edge of the rainforests lining the Padas River while the latter is a fun ride along part of the same track combining the thrill of a steam train trip with a nostalgic experience.

The departure of the NBR is timed at a civilized 10 a.m. so that the mostly foreign tourists have ample time to fuel themselves over breakfast at the various resort hotels lining the Kota Kinabalu foreshore.

The steam train is fuelled by local baku logs sourced from mangrove forests to propel it along the narrow, rickety, train line. There is a suggestion that it is one of the few trains left in the world that is still fuelled by wood.

The NBR provides comfortable surroundings in renovated carriages which are opulent and indulgent compared to the local train. Many travel on the North Borneo Railway for its convenience while others appear to simply enjoy the fun of a bygone era. There is something appealing in the romance of steam train travel as it conjures up images of a near-forgotten past and of a very relaxed and civilized mode of transportation.

Above: The steam train rolls through the Sabah forests with its whistle blasting to warm motorists traversing minor road crossings to get out of its way.

The railway is a joint venture begun in 2000 between Sutera Harbour Resort and the Sabah State Railway. Trains can accommodate 80 passengers in five, fully renovated, colonial-style carriages pulled by a 90-ton (82-tonne) Vulcan steam engine made by the Vulcan Foundry Ltd in Newton-le-Willows, Lancashire, England. It successfully recreates an era when the state was known as British North Borneo. Then, the train offered a life-line for the people who lived in this part of Sabah and, even today, it still serves a valuable function carrying people and goods to and from Tenom (the train originally went further north-west to the town of Malalap but this section was subsequently abandoned).

Passengers can get an idea of the days of the British North Borneo Chartered Company and the British Colonial Office, when young Englishmen set out on a tropical adventure as planters and plantation managers in the mystical Far East. Typically, they would have been young men heading off on the railway into the wilds of the dense jungle in search of adventure and riches beyond their wildest imagination.

The line runs from Tanjung Aru through the township of Kinarut on its way to Papar. A Buddhist temple in Kinarut is the first stop of several along the way and being a very colourful Buddhist structure, most tourists enjoy the opportunity to make a closer inspection while the local children seem amused at the interest shown in something that is so everyday to them.

With a flourish of whistle blowing, the train heads off and passes through mangrove swamps and rice fields where water buffaloes meander in the paddies lining the track. Small roads cross the line and the train driver works overtime on the whistle to warn motorists to get out of the way.

The train crosses the Papar River over a steel trestle bridge into Papar where the train stops for 40 minutes for passengers to experience this 'rice bowl' township and the local market (called a *tamu* in this part of the world). Rice is a staple in the diet of most Malaysians and is grown around the small town. While the passengers enjoy the market, the train is turned on a huge rotating wheel ready for the return journey.

Below: At Papar, the steam engine is rotated in readiness for the return journey.

On the return journey, drinks and lunch are served by a crew of enthusiastic, young, pith-helmeted stewards. Lunch is delivered in traditional tiffin boxes as it would have been in the colonial days. This unique culinary experience highlights the exotic blend of Asian and Western styles but with an emphasis on several popular Malaysian delights. Wines and beers are served at a reasonable price. The free flow of lemon squash is most welcome as the open windows keep the temperature quite warm. Ceiling fans whir away and maintain the authenticity of the colonial era prior to the concept of air-conditioning. The train arrives back at 1.40 p.m.

Each exterior and interior of the carriages has been refurbished in the style of a typical 19th century train. The exterior is painted in the traditional deep green and cream and brass logos feature the original design of a tiger standing on the royal crown while holding a rail wheel.

SABAH STATE RAILWAY

For many villagers the train line to Tenom was the only way for them to access the remote Padas Valley. In days gone by, the railway opened up the area but now roads provide quicker access to the outside world for the people of Tenom. The railway was begun by William C. Cowrie, Chairman of the British North Borneo Chartered Company.

The local train is recommended for 'trainspotters' who see this unique journey as something to tick off on the list of the world's most exotic train journeys. The public train is not only cheap but one full of character and characters. It can take up to six hours to reach its destination and delays are not uncommon. The recommended journey is to take the 87-mile (140-km) long train ride to Tenom, spend the night there (there is an excellent agricultural research station with an extensive selection of tropical plants), then catch the train back to civilization the next day. Coffee is also grown in Tenom and sampling the local brew is an essential activity while in the town.

These pages: Alaska Railroad's flagship passenger train, Denali Star, routinely carries specially appointed cruise train cars for tour operators, such as Princess Tours.

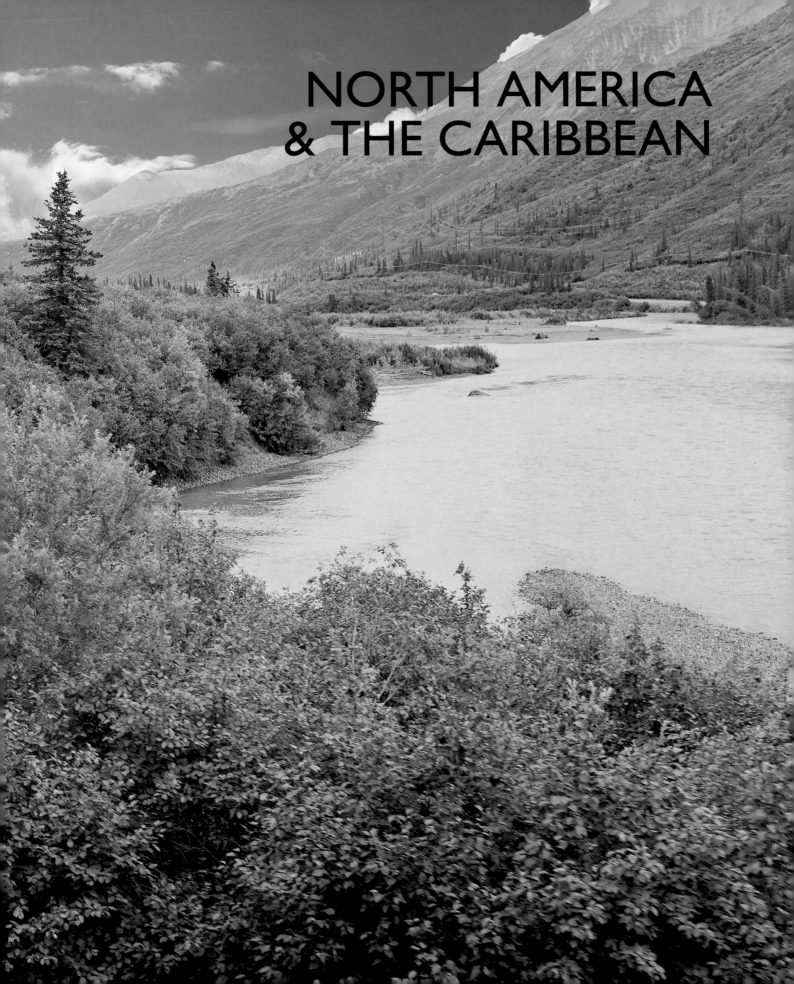

NORTH AMERICA
& THE CARIBBEAN

THE ALASKA RAILROAD
A Rolling Panorama of Stunning Natural Beauty

BRIAN SOLOMON

Among the most interesting and most unusual American railroads is the famed Alaska Railroad that exclusively operates within its namesake state. Although the United States purchased Alaska territory from Czarist Russia in 1867, it was slow to settle the newly acquired region. It is separated from the continental United States by Canada's province of British Columbia. Popularly known as 'The Last Frontier,' only in 1959 was Alaska admitted as a state,

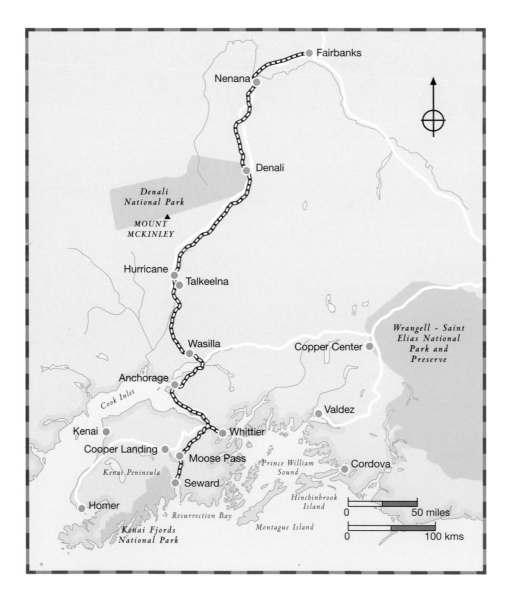

the 49th of 50. By land area Alaska is the largest state encompassing 664,988 sq miles (1,722,311 sq km), yet, with slightly more than 710,000 people, it is among the smallest by population. Not only is much of Alaska exceptionally remote, but it's also a rugged and wild land of exceptional natural beauty featuring 17 of the 20 tallest mountains in the United States. Denali (Mt McKinley) is the tallest in North America, rising to an altitude of 20,320 feet (6,193 m).

The Alaska Railroad is not typical of American railways. It was largely built during the 20th century and, while most American lines have been privately constructed and operated, the majority of the Alaska Railroad route was built by the federal government, and federally operated until 1985 when the state of Alaska bought it. It is physically isolated from the rest of the North American network, and its freight interchange requires car ferries from Whittier to Seattle to access the lower 48 states. Also, unlike most American railroads which conveyed long-distance passenger operations to Amtrak in the 1970s, Alaska has continued to run its own passenger trains and does so with a degree of style rarely found in the lower 48. Its network consists of roughly 535 route miles (573 km) with its main trunk running north from Seward via Anchorage to Fairbanks. There are a few branches, including the line via the road/rail Anton Anderson Memorial Tunnel to the Prince William Sound ferry port at Whittier.

The Alaska Railroad is a vital freight and passenger artery, and its passenger trains remain popular with tourists. Alaska residents are encouraged to ride with

Above: Alaska Railroad's Denali Star crosses the massive truss bridge over the Tanana River near Nenana, Alaska. This impressive span is one of the railroad's most significant pieces of infrastructure.

Overleaf: Late summer is one of the best times to visit Alaska. The weather tends to be drier and the days are still long. Alaska Railroad is unusual in its assignment of modern SD70MAC diesels to passenger trains. In this view a SD70MAC and GP40-2 work together on the southbound Denali Star at Ester.

a 20 per cent discount on fares. The railroad cooperates with cruise ship companies and handles special cars with upmarket accommodation for tour groups on its regularly scheduled trains. While tours are one way to experience Alaska by rail, the railroad's own cars accept fare-paying passengers.

Alaska is abundant with wildlife; passengers may spot moose, bear and occasionally wolves from the train. Mountainous panoramas and vistas of glaciers are among the scenes that attract thousands of train riders annually.

While it is possible to travel over most of Alaska Railroad's mainline, no one train covers the full length of the run. As of the summer 2014 season, the railroad typically operates four services. The *Denali Star* is Alaska's flagship train, which runs daily between mid May and mid September on the 356 miles (573 km) between Anchorage and Fairbanks. It departs Anchorage northbound at 8.15 a.m. and normally takes just under 12 hours. On its way it stops at Wasilla and Talkeetna, the latter a town noted for its exceptional scenery and its mayor, which at last report was a cat. It also stops at Denali to serve passengers visiting Denali National Park. This is a popular layover point, where visitors may embark on a variety of thrilling outdoor adventures. The southbound *Denali Star* departs Fairbanks at 8.15 a.m. with an expected arrival in Anchorage at 8 p.m. The two trains meet at a halfway point. Holland America/Westours McKinley, Princess Tours and Royal Celebrity tours routinely operate cars on the *Denali Star*.

For a completely different experience from the upscale cruise trains, which may appeal to more intrepid railway enthusiasts, consider Alaska Railroad's *Hurricane Turn*. This starts at Talkeetna at 12.45 p.m. providing a local stopping service to remote areas, and typically reaches Hurricane by 3 p.m. where it lays over for an hour before heading south again. It is used by local residents, sportsmen and railroad employees to reach regions inaccessible by road.

Although the entire Alaska Railroad is famous for its stunning views of the landscape, the line south from Anchorage is especially dramatic. The *Coastal Classic* runs between Anchorage and Seward. This departs Anchorage southbound at 6.45 a.m., stops at Girdwood between 8.50 and 8.55 a.m., and arrives at Seward just after 11 a.m. Northbound it leaves Seward for a 10.15 p.m. arrival at Anchorage. This runs in the long days from the second week of May to mid September, so despite its relatively late arrival at Anchorage, most of the run is in daylight.

The *Glacier Discovery* runs south from Anchorage to Whittier, featuring several scenic stops. This begins operation in early June and runs through to mid September. On the branch to Whittier it passes through two tunnels.

During the colder, darker months, when the other passenger services are in hibernation (along with a lot of the wildlife) Alaska Railroad runs its *Aurora Winter* train at weekends (and selected mid-winter weekdays) between Fairbanks and Anchorage.

THE QUEBEC, NORTH SHORE & LABRADOR

A Ride into the Wilderness

BRIAN SOLOMON

I n 1950, the Quebec, North Shore & Labrador (QNS&L) began construction of an all-new railway, physically isolated from the rest of the North American network, with the primary purpose of tapping iron ore reserves in the Canadian

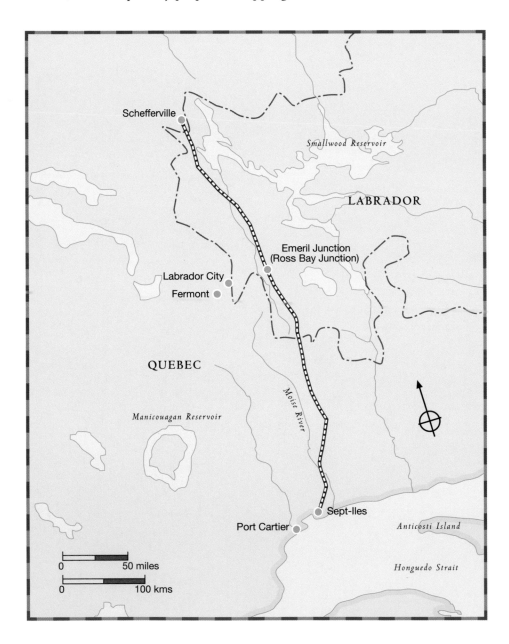

Shield in Labrador and northern Quebec and transporting them to ports on the Gulf of St Lawrence. This line was cut through wilderness and remains one of the most remote railways in North America. The primary route extends inland from the north shore of the Gulf of St Lawrence at Sept Îles (Seven Islands), Quebec, northwards 357 miles (575 km) to Schefferville, Quebec, via Labrador. An important branch runs from Emeril Junction (Ross Bay Junction) to Labrador City. Since 1982, ore originating at open pit mines near Labrador City has supplied the bulk of revenue on the line.

Historically, QNS&L operated freight and passenger services. Its freight trains are the heaviest in North America and among the largest of any regularly operated in the world. Ore trains consisting of up to 265 freight cars can weigh up to 33,700 short tons (based on 2,000 lb/907 kg), nearly twice that of a typical North American mineral train. These are run with multiple sets of modern high-horse-power locomotives, not just at the front of the train but spread across the consist at strategic places, and operated using state-of-the-art distributed power technology that allows precision, synchronized control by the locomotive engineer.

QNS&L upgraded its passenger service in 1994 with the purchase of second-hand Budd RDCs from Canada's VIA Rail. These served for about a decade until they were replaced with more modern equipment. At the end of 2005, newly formed Tshiuetin Rail Transportation Incorporated (TRT) assumed control of the QNS&L line north from the junction at Emeril, including operation of passenger

Below: The maiden voyage of Quebec, North Shore & Labrador's re-equipped passenger train in June 2001. This features classic, lightweight, streamlined passenger cars, typical of those used on North American railroads from the 1930s to the 1970s.

services on the Sept Îles—Schefferville route. (Although passenger services traditionally operated via a branch directly to Labrador City as well, as of 2014 only the main line was served.) The owners of Tshiuetin are described on the company website as three groups of aboriginal First Nations: Innu Takuaikan Uashat Mak Mani-Utenam, Naskapi Nation of Kawawachikamach and Nation Innu Matimekush–Lac John. These represent many of the local people in the region who travel on the company's passenger trains. The name Tshiuetin is translated as 'north wind.'

In 2014, TRT was advertising two runs weekly, with trains departing Sept Îles at 8 a.m. for the northbound run on Mondays and Thursday, and Schefferville at noon on Tuesdays and Fridays. Running time end to end is estimated at about seven hours, but owing to the importance of iron-ore traffic and the exceptionally remote operation, actual transit times may vary. Advance booking is advised.

The train ride brings passengers into true wilderness. Over most of the line there are no roads and no towns. Tom Carver, a colleague who travelled the route, explained, "except for the railroad itself and the occasional power line, the hand of man is rarely seen from the train". The railway is so isolated that helicopters are used to transport train crews and maintenance personnel. Most of the line is dispatched remotely from Sept Îles using a centralized traffic control (CTC) system that allows dispatchers to set the track switches at passing sidings and authorize train movements by signal indication. However, in the event of a signal failure or related difficulty, signal maintainers are sent in by chopper. The helicopters must closely follow the line so if they run into problems they can be reached easily.

Almost immediately after departing Sept Îles, the line follows the east bank of the Moisie River. This traverses a deep, wild and wonderful canyon, a view which Carver described as "despite its location in eastern Canada, is on a scale more like scenery found in Alberta or British Columbia". On the lower portions of the route, the line passes dense coniferous forests that abound with wildlife: moose, bear, deer and birds can be seen from the train.

Further north the scenery changes, and becomes what the Russians describe as 'taiga', which is boreal coniferous forest characterized by evergreen trees, bushes, lichen and other small plants, with water everywhere in the form of rivers, streams, lakes and ponds. This scenery is common across much of Canada's northern regions and similar to that found in Alaska, Russian Siberia and Scandinavia.

Winters are brutal and summers can bring days of torrential rain, but in the warmer months, when the rain finally passes, clear blue skies reveal pristine landscapes, fresh air and an escape from all the problems of modern living.

There is some tourism at Labrador City. Carver said, "Lab City is a great place, the people are friendly, there's some fantastic restaurants, and the mine tour was excellent. They brought us into where they were dumping ore, which was fascinating." Sportsmen can enjoy fishing, and tours specialize in bringing fishermen to remote areas using float planes that can land on water.

Below: Labrador offers a mix of taiga and crystalline virgin lakes, scenery unspoiled by the hand of man.

THE ADIRONDACK SCENIC RAILROAD
A Railroad Returned from Near Oblivion

BRIAN SOLOMON

T he Adirondack Scenic Railroad is like Washington Irving's story *Rip Van Winkle*; the line having slept for decades has awoken to a changed world. Where some railroads are alive, and others were abandoned and lifted, the Adirondack line between Utica and Lake Placid lay dormant for years, its tracks intact but unused, nature gradually encroaching. Since the 1990s, portions

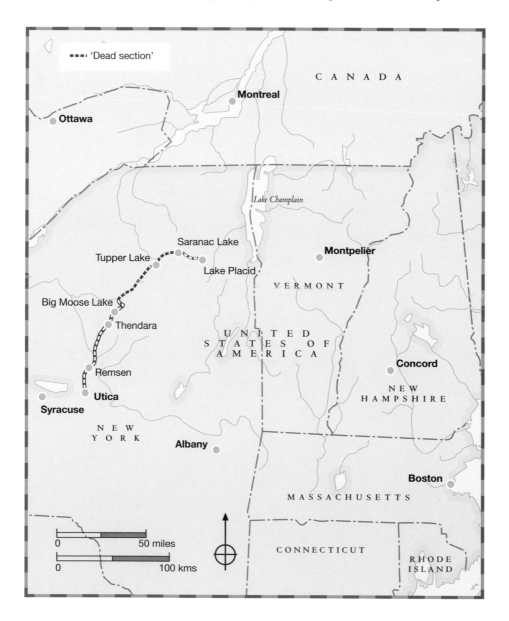

of the line have been reactivated and there is again seasonal excursion service from some of the towns on the route, yet long stretches of track still remain quiet.

Above: Adirondack Scenic's excursion train at Lake Placid on an evocative autumn evening.

The railway's isolation, its long slumber and scenic areas traversed put it among the most unusual routes in the north-eastern United States. Perhaps the most compelling element of the railroad is its 'dead section' that reaches deep into the Adirondack wilderness. Although this line remains closed (as of 2015), when travelling Adirondack Scenic's trains, the rider knows the line goes much further, like taking an exploratory step into a vast cavern, the daylight rapidly drops away revealing only hints of the inky depths beyond.

The name Adirondack is derived from Native American words that mean 'tree eater' or 'bark eater' and refers to the people of this forested region who some-times subsisted on the bark of trees. It is one of the least populated parts of the eastern United States. This extremely scenic area is dominated by Adirondack Park, covering some six million acres (2,428,113 ha), making it the largest of its kind in the continental United States and the largest wilderness area in the East. The park was created in 1892, the same year that Dr William Seward Webb, 'Seward' to his close associates, opened the region's most important railway lines.

Webb was a trained surgeon who skilfully married into one of America's most powerful railroad families. His wife, Lila Osgood Vanderbilt, was daughter of William Henry Vanderbilt, head of the New York Central, and granddaughter of the railroad's famous founder, Cornelius 'Commodore' Vanderbilt. Although both of the senior Vanderbilt's had died by the time Webb began his railroad, the Vanderbilt family remained at the helm of New York Central, which was one of the two most powerful lines in the eastern United States (the other being the Pennsylvania Railroad).

Alvin Harlow in his book, *Road of the Century*, explains that Webb began his penetration of the Adirondacks by taking control of a narrow gauge line running north from New York Central's main artery at Herkimer and blending it with a new company called the St Lawrence & Adirondack. He built rapidly, running his route north from Remsen, via Thendara, over a summit at Big Moose Lake to Tupper Lake, and northwards towards Montreal. A secondary route was built to Ottawa. Among Webb's incentives was to make this remote region more accessible to wealthy tourists interested in hunting and fishing.

Although effectively part of the Vanderbilt empire from its beginning, in the early 20th century this was melded into the vast New York Central System and functioned as the railroad's primary route for Montreal traffic. The line thrived, serving as an important route for the forestry industry and for through traffic to Canada, as well as hosting through passenger trains from New York's Grand Central Terminal and from Buffalo to Montreal, while serving communities along the line, and resort areas such as Saranac Lake and Lake Placid. As late as 1945, three passenger trains in each direction traversed the length of the route daily between Utica and Montreal, with connections via local trains for Saranac Lake and Lake Placid. Decline set in after the war. The last regularly scheduled New York Central passenger trains ran in 1965, and while the line remained open for freight until 1972, it wasn't included as part of Conrail and was taken over by the state of New York after 1975. In 1980, the route was briefly revived, when a company called the Adirondack Railway was contracted by New York to provide service from Utica to Lake Placid in conjunction with the 1980 Winter Olympic Games. In 1981, service concluded and the line was left derelict.

In 1992 an isolated four-mile (6.5 km) section at Thendara, New York, was reopened for limited excursion service. In 1993, the entire route north from Remsen to Lake Placid was listed on the National Register of Historic Places which helped preserve it. Over the last 20 years, Adirondack Scenic has gradually restored portions of the route for passenger excursion. Operations are based at Utica, where passengers can transfer to Amtrak trains for other New York cities, at Thendara and at Lake Placid, resorts in the heart of the Adirondack region. Most recently, the line north of Thendara (near Old Forge) was reopened to the summit at Big Moose Lake, 2,035 feet (620 m) above sea level. This involves a steady climb up a sinuous 2.2 per cent gradient. It is now possible to take seasonal excursions on the lower 63 miles (101 km) between Utica and Big Moose, and on the upper ten miles (16 km) between Lake Placid and Saranac Lake.

Riding north from Utica, the first few miles of line are shared with Mohawk, Adirondack & Northern, a freight railroad operated by Genesee Valley Transportation. Not far out of Utica, signs of population dwindle away and a sense of wilderness closes in. The landscape becomes a blur of forest, with only the occasional hint at civilization in the form of a grade crossing or a house along the line. At Remsen, a few sidings, the station and broad area are all that remains of the important yard and junction active here in the line's heyday. The old narrow gauge route from Herkimer came up from the south. A few miles north is Snow

Below: An historic former New York Central Alco RS-3 dressed in the vintage lightning stripe paint livery leads an Adirondack Scenic excursion south of Thendara, New York.

Junction, where MA&N's line continues on its path to reach freight customers. Eight miles (12.5 km) beyond Remsen is Forestport, where the old station looks like something invented by Stephen King for the setting of a gothic story.

The miles of forested line make for an enigmatic journey. The Adirondack region is famous for storms, and the journey may be greeted by a sudden deluge, where waves of water accompanied by thunder and lightning add a sense of adventure. While pleasant in the summer, the best time to ride is in early autumn, when the foliage is at its brightest. The Adirondacks are blessed with one of the longest and most brilliant foliage seasons in the eastern United States, and the train remains one of the best ways to see the region's remotest areas.

Adirondack Scenic's middle 70-mile (113 km) 'dead section' remains an elusive journey only traversed by rare equipment moves and made by railroad employees. Recently, Chicago-based Iowa Pacific Holdings, an active operator of short line railroads, rail passenger excursions and passenger trains, has expressed interest in operating through Pullman cars directly from New York City to Lake Placid over the length of the Adirondack Scenic's line north from Utica. While many people in the region would delight in the eventual reopening of the line, a

Above: Adirondack Scenic's former Alaska Railroad 1508 is an F7A diesel built by General Motors' Electro-Motive Division at LaGrange, Illinois. In the 1950s this was among the most common locomotives in North America. It leads a southbound summer excursion train at Thendara, New York.

small but vocal group of selfish obstructionists have been lobbying to lift the tracks and close the line forever. Hopefully, this route that has survived so long, will remain on the map for generations to come, and the elusive journeys through the forests and mountains of the Adirondacks will again be open for all to enjoy.

Left: There is something eerie and compelling about the Adirondack's 'dead section', so rarely travelled, making it a mysterious, elusive, rusty path through the wilderness, yet someday it may carry passengers again.

THE CALIFORNIA WESTERN
Lonely Tracks through the Redwoods

BRIAN SOLOMON

C alifornia's rugged coast north of San Francisco offered the perfect environment for one of the world's most magnificent forests. For centuries
the California coastal redwood Sequoias flourished and were the tallest
living things. Western settlers arrived, awed by California's natural resources, less
excited by its stunning beauty than by its potential riches. It should be no surprise that settlers, characterized by the gold-rush buccaneers, soon eyed the great
redwood forests as a resource to be exploited.

Redwoods were among California's defining materials in the late 19th and
early 20th centuries. This wood was ideal for building the elaborate 'ginger-
bread' Victorian architecture styles that came to characterize Californian cities. As
San Francisco boomed in the second half of the 19th century, redwood houses
sprouted up on its famous hills.

The forests to the north offered an ample supply of timber, with giant Sequoias
reaching as high as 375 feet (114 m) tall and up to 23 feet (7 m) in diameter at

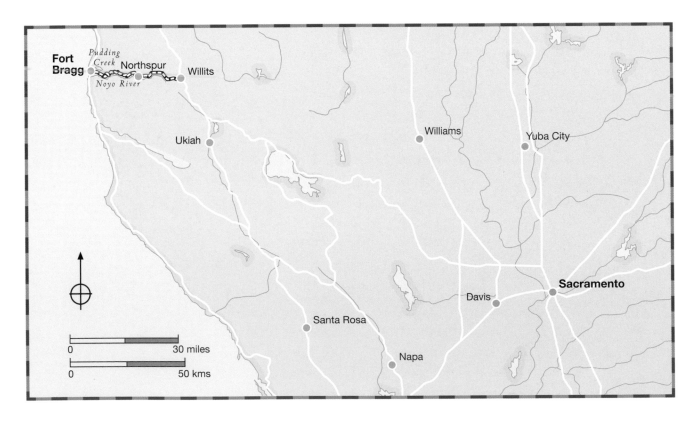

Left: *The railway ride through the world's tallest trees is like none other. But, remember, the tall trees growing today are all second and third growth. The really big trees were all cut down decades ago and only their stumps remain.*

the base of the trunk. One of the places that benefited from the logging trade was the old military outpost at Fort Bragg, located where Pudding Creek and the Noyo River flowed into the vast Pacific. Its name is ironic; it had been named in honour of West Point graduate Captain Brixton Bragg in 1857, just a few years before the American Civil War erupted, with him on the Confederate side. Among the side effects of that bloody conflict was authorization for the Pacific Railroad to link California with the East (specifically, the Union). The two companies building America's first Transcontinental line were the California-based Central Pacific working east and Union Pacific working west.

Ultimately, railroading enriched California; San Francisco in particular flour-ished, fuelling a building boom. The Fort Bragg Railroad was built in 1885 to link

coastal timber mills with the timber stands along Pudding Creek. It was similar to other isolated timber railroads across northern Cal-ifornia. Yet, this line proved unusual. Where most lines did little more than connect timber stands with small coastal ports, the railroad rooted at Fort Bragg pushed further inland than most. Its builders penetrated the upper Noyo Valley boring a 1,184-foot (361-m) tun-nel under the ridge dividing the Pudding Creek and Noyo River watersheds. In 1905 it was renamed in 1905 the California Western Railroad & Navigation Company. Its timber trade flourished following the Great San Fran-cisco Earthquake and Fire of 1906, which de-stroyed much of the city and spurred a second, unparalleled building boom. By 1911, the line had continued over the Coast Range to reach a connection with the recently built North-western Pacific at Willits, giving it an all-rail connection to the Bay Area. Thus the Califor-nia Western matured from a mere timber rail-road to a full service, common carrier line.

Regularly scheduled passenger service began in 1912. For a brief period in the 1920s CW carried through sleeping cars in cooper-ation with Northwestern Pacific, linking Fort

Bragg with the Bay Area. (Passengers for San Francisco needed to make the final few miles via a ferry connection from Sausalito.)

However, passenger trains were expensive to run, and in 1925 the railroad made the decision to cut costs by introducing a petrol-fuelled railbus in place of steam-hauled trains. While such a move was consistent with many branch lines of the period, the railcar made a doubly lasting impact on California Western. Exhaust from primitive gasoline engines irritated the sensitive nostrils of Californians adapted to fresh Pacific breezes and clean mountain air, so CW's newfangled railcars were compared to the odiferous skunks that inhabited the forests. The cars became known as 'Skunk trains'. The nickname stuck and evolved as a theme to the railroad's popular passenger service. By the 1950s, when most railroads had retired their pre-war gasoline railcars, CW's remained and the railroad gained fame as a result. A stylized cartoon skunk emerged as the line's mascot.

Through the 1970s, nocturnal freights remained as the railroad's bread and butter, but the economy changed and its once-lucrative timber traffic waned. By the

Below: In 1966, California Western was still a common carrier. Its 'Skunk train' railcars met Northwestern Pacific's tri-weekly Budd-rail diesel car at Willits, California. NWP's RDC was discontinued in 1971 on the eve of Amtrak. California Western car 300, pictured, was built by Brill for Seaboard Air Line, and later converted from gas-electric to diesel-electric operation. It is similar to cars built for operation in Cuba.

1990s, the line was only moving a few hundred cars annually. Then in 1998, the NWP route was closed which cut CW off from the rest of the American freight network. The same year the old timber mill at Fort Bragg shut. By this time, the railroad had adapted into a tourist line, using both its historic 'Skunk' cars and locomotive-hauled trains. Its passenger services had also evolved from traditional scheduled trains serving online communities to an excursion service for visiting tourists to view the tall trees.

Today, excursion trains work from both ends of the line, and most trains turn on the wheel at the midway point called Northspur, a forest oasis deep among the Redwoods far from towns and highways. Owing to the difficult terrain, the railroad requires a 40-mile (64-km) line, following Pudding Creek and Noyo Rivers and over the Coast Range, to traverse just 23 miles (37 km) as the crow flies. Most of the journey is inaccessible by road so passengers are given views only obtainable by rail. The trip from Fort Bragg winds inland on a largely water-level route, while travellers from Willits are treated to a more mountainous line, which ascends from 1,364 feet (416 m) to the summit at 1,740 feet (530 m), then down a steep 3.5 per cent gradient, looping and turning through a series of tight (23 degree) curves which produce 8½ miles (13.5 km) of line on a spaghetti-like path spanning just 1½ miles (2.5 km) of a direct line.

Above: California Western's mascot is a skunk in a railroad hat and overalls. The railroad's famous 'Skunk trains' were gas-electric railcars that earned their nickname because of their stinky internal combustion exhaust.

The towering redwood trees are the line's attraction. Yet, visitors should not mistake these forest giants for the trees that attracted the railroad's builders more than a century ago. Almost all of the original trees were harvested and sawn up decades ago. The trees that grow along the line today are second and third growth. The historic trees were much larger, leading to speculation that the climatic conditions that fostered their vast proportions have changed. In the forest, vast stumps with a diameter of more than a dozen feet (3.5 m) remain as ghostly reminders of the original trunks. The trees that are growing today aren't merely the descendants of the original trees, they are, in fact, sprouts from the old roots! Although cut for their timber, the redwoods rejuvenate, and often new shoots will ring the massive, decapitated stump of a harvested tree.

Perhaps the final irony is that 'The Redwood Route' — as the California Western was known before its 'Skunk trains' became famous — survives, so that visitors can enjoy views of the new trees that grew in place of those once harvested for the line's freight traffic. The railroad, like the forest, has adapted to this new reality.

THE SOUTH SHORE
America's Last Interurban Electric

BRIAN SOLOMON

Once upon a time a century ago, lightly built, interurban electric railways connected cities and towns all across the United States. The midwestern states were blessed with an especially dense network of electric lines, which ran through city streets, along the sides of roads, across the open fields and often parallel with the older, more established, 'steam railroads'. Before the advent of paved highways and the proliferation of automobiles and buses, interurban trains afforded good transportation, which supplemented, and often competed with, steam lines for passenger and freight traffic.

Electric interurbans flourished only briefly, reaching their zenith before the First World War. The advent of the automotive industry doomed these colourful railways. They began to vanish in the 1920s, and many succumbed during the Great Depression, so by the 1950s there were only a few lines left. In some places fragments of the old interurbans were integrated into the railroad network, and today only one true interurban line survives as a passenger carrier: the famed Chicago, South Shore & South Bend, known universally as the 'South Shore'.

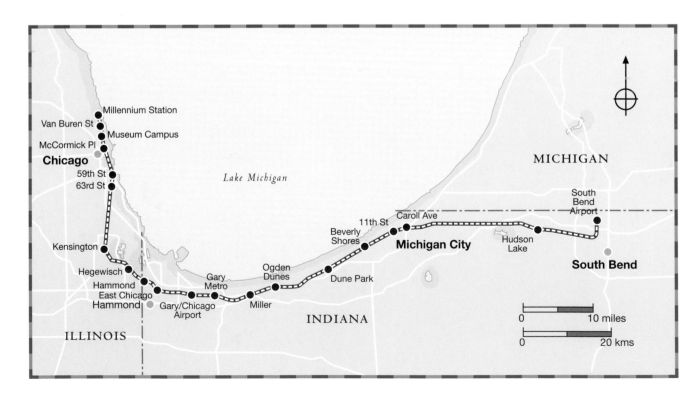

This line isn't exotic because of the terrain it traverses or the curious towns it connects, its charm stems from the fact that it is the very last of its breed, having outlived all of its contemporaries, surviving into the modern era. While the South Shore is familiar to railway enthusiasts, too often it has been ignored by world travellers who are either oblivious of its unusual status, or dismissive of the territory it serves. Yet it received a listing in Thomas Cook's Overseas Timetable, and has been the topic of books and magazine articles over the years.

Historically, South Shore was one of three large interurban systems serving Chicago, all of which benefited from the ownership and management of Samuel Insull, who also headed the city's rapid transit system and electric power company. Insull bought control of Chicago, Lake Shore & South Bend in 1925 and renamed it Chicago, South Shore & South Bend Railroad. By 1926, he had improved its electrification and introduced direct electric service to downtown Chicago over Illinois Central's suburban lines.

Above: Just after sunset, a South Shore train races along its electrified single track across the open fields of northern Indiana. Interurban electric lines once covered the American Midwest, today South Shore is the last interurban electric passenger line.

Although the Depression ended Insull's control, all three of his railways retained good ridership figures through the Second World War. South Shore underwent various changes over the decades, but by the 1970s its passenger service, like many across North America, was no longer profitable; the line paid its bills with freight traffic while continuing to run its old electrics.

In 1977, the Northern Indiana Commuter Transportation District was created to preserve South Shore as a passenger route, then in 1982 new Japanese-built stainless steel cars were bought to replace the tired and well-travelled Insull-era electric cars. NICTD began direct passenger operations in 1989, with a separate private company acquiring the freight operations (operated as South Shore Freight). Both passenger and freight operations retain the insignia and traction orange-and-maroon colour scheme of the traditional South Shore. In 2009, South Shore expanded its fleet with some double-deck electric cars.

South Shore retains elements of the classic North American interurban electric railway and yet serves as a regular passenger carrier. At 90 miles (145 km) in length, it has one of the longest runs operated by a North American suburban railway, and some of its trains provide an intercity function by virtue of its length.

Passenger trains run from Chicago's Millennium Station using Metra's Electric District former Illinois Central line to Kensington Tower, where it diverges onto its own right-of-way. The route then runs east through heavily industrialized areas to Gary, Indiana, and past the famous dunes on Indiana's Lake Michigan shore (which earned it the nickname 'Duneland Electric') to Michigan City. Over much of its route South Shore runs adjacent to heavily travelled mainline railways. One

Left: Today South Shore freights are diesel hauled. An Electro-Motive Division GP38-2 works at Burns Harbour, Indiana.

of the highlights of South Shore's classic operation is through Michigan City where it runs right down the middle of the street on a hill and dale profile — a characteristic of old-time interurban lines. The railway continues east on a single track through agricultural lands towards South Bend. In recent years an extension has connected South Shore to the South Bend Airport. Frequent services connect Chicago and Michigan City with approximately 18 round trips daily; however, the most interesting portion of the railway on the far east end only sees five weekday round trips. A round trip from Chicago to South Bend makes for a good day's outing and allows visitors to fully experience America's last interurban.

FERROCARRILES DE CUBA
Cuba's Railway Paradise

BRIAN SOLOMON

Cuba is the largest of the Caribbean Islands, measuring more than 780 miles (1,255 km) long, and located less than 100 miles (160 km) from Florida on the American mainland. The capital, Havana, lies on the north coast, south-west of Key West. The Cuban landscape is characterized by lush fertile lowlands that for centuries have been used for the cultivation of sugar cane. Sugar was traditionally one of Cuba's chief exports and a primary reason for its intensive railway development.

Cuba adopted the railway in 1837, earlier than many countries in continental Europe. In its heyday, Cuban railroads were among the most densely developed networks in the world, and comprised the most intensive railway network in Latin America. Today it is the only significant Caribbean network remaining.

Private companies were responsible for the construction of an extensive common carrier system that at its peak extended over more than 3,640 route miles (5,858 km). Even more comprehensive were the networks of industrial railways

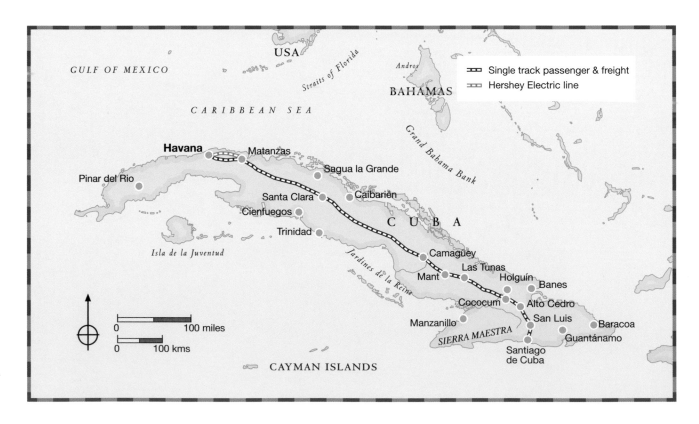

- ▭▭▭ Single track passenger & freight
- ▭▭▭ Hershey Electric line

built to serve the sugar plantations, many of them narrow gauge, which at their zenith consisted of more than 7,500 route miles (12,070 km).

Cuba's railway paradise has attracted visitors for more than 50 years, largely because of the unusual conditions that stemmed from the 1959 revolution and subsequent events that brought Fidel Castro's government to power, and Cuba's on-going estranged relations with the United States due to its controversial alignment with the Soviet Eastern bloc. Its unusual political situation contributed to economic conditions with the effect of freezing Cuba's railways in a time warp. For decades this resulted in the continued operation of steam locomotives in regular service and the maintaining of throwbacks, such as the Hershey Cuban Railroad's electric interurban lines, which retained many of the attributes of a 1920s American rural electric railway.

While Cuba's railways have declined from their peak, the continued operation of passenger trains with antiquated equipment, plus the great variety of international locomotives and cars combined with traditional operations, make it one of the most world's most interesting places to ride and photograph trains.

Although they are less well known outside of Cuba than the famous Hershey Electric (see page 104), Cuba's mainline railways continue to operate long-distance passenger services including overnight trains.

In the 1920s, several of Cuba's common carrier railways were combined into the United Railways of Havana, while others were operated as the Consolidated Railroads of Cuba. The railways were controlled by foreigners; the chairman of the board and other top officials of United Railways were based in London, while corporate offices for the Consolidated were in New York's Grand Central Terminal. Prior to the 1959 revolution, Cuban railways tended to purchase most of their equipment from American manufacturers, with Baldwin and Alco steam locomotives being standard on both common carrier lines and sugar-plantation railroads. During the 1950s, Consolidated followed the American example of modernization with the purchase of new General Motors diesel-electric locomotives and Budd Company's Rail Diesel Cars (RDCs).

Nationalization began prior to the revolution. In 1952, United Railways were transformed into a state-run organization called Ferrocarriles Occidentales de Cuba (Western Railroads of Cuba). Under Castro, the common carriers were merged into the state-run Ferrocarilles de Cuba (National Railways of Cuba or Cuban National Railways) which continues its operations to the present.

The mainline runs from Havana's Estación Central (Central Station) east via Matanzas, Santa Clara and Camagüey, to Santiago de Cuba, a distance of 531 miles (854 km). While travellers should be advised that Cuban trains aren't maintained to European standards, the best trains on this route use second-hand, stainless-steel body carriages from France equipped with air-conditioning, although this doesn't always work as intended. Train speeds vary, and it takes up to 18 hours to make the full run.

Purchasing railway tickets can be complicated as the result of a dual economy,

Below: Imported diesel locomotives are seen shunting freight cars near FCC's Estación Central in Havana.

whereby Cubans and foreigners need to play by different rules. Not only do foreigners need to pay for tickets with convertible pesos (a currency specifically designed for foreigners, known as 'CUC'), but foreigners also cannot expect to queue with the locals at Estación Central in Havana. Instead they need to buy tickets in the old La Courbe Station building around the corner. Non-nationals should expect to pay substantially higher prices for tickets than locals, which is true of many goods and services in Cuba. The bureaucracy of purchasing tickets appears to emulate the Soviet prototype. Even a simple ticket requires a time-consuming bureaucratic ordeal involving considerable thumping and stamping of paperwork.

Cuban railways are one of the few places in the world where American, European, Russian and Chinese-built equipment coexist. The mainline network still moves freight as well as passenger trains.

Experiences riding mainline trains have varied: a colleague, Donncha Cronin, reported that he was strongly discouraged from travelling by train and urged to take the bus instead! Other reports indicate foreigners are dissuaded from travelling by train because of crowded conditions and comparatively poor accommodation. Despite this, the intrepid railway enthusiast may still wish to take a cross-country trip on Cuban intercity trains for the chance to do something few foreigners experience.

THE HERSHEY ELECTRIC
Built to Convey Chocolate

BRIAN SOLOMON

Some names are so evocative that they stick, despite being obsolete for decades. Take, for example, the Hershey Electric. Beginning in 1916, the Hershey Cuban Railroad was built by the American chocolate company to supply sugar and other materials to candy factories as well as providing transport back to Havana harbour. Yet from its early days it served as both a freight and passenger line.

Hershey electrified after the First World War, and its operation assumed the characteristics of a classic North American interurban trolley line, similar to the Chicago, South Shore & South Bend (described on pages 96 to 99). This endeared it to railway enthusiasts who delighted in its chocolate-coloured cars bouncing along on lightly built infrastructure complete with street-trackage and road-side running.

Below: A few of the old Brill interurban cars survive on the Hershey Electric. Although modernized with new windows and other equipment, the guts of these cars date back more than 90 years.

Left: The Hershey cars are well patronized, mostly by local people who rely on the service for regional transportation. Tourists enjoy the quaint electric line, which is reminiscent of early 20th century trolley lines in the United States and Canada.

Below: A view from the front of a Hershey Electric car as it bobs along in the countryside east of Havana. Like many things in Cuba, the old electric line survives out of necessity with minimal maintenance.

Hershey has survived for decades after most classic American interurban lines all but vanished from the scene. At its peak, Hershey operated about 109 miles (176 km). It survives as a common carrier running from Havana to Matanzas, with about 91 miles (147 km) of line as well as some short branches in the vicinity of Hershey itself. Although the railway lost its affiliation with Hershey Company many years ago, and under the Castro-regime was nationalized in 1960 becoming the Camilo Cienfuegos Division, the old name survives.

A few passenger services are still conducted with antique, 1920s-vintage, Brill electric cars built in Philadelphia. In the late 1990s, to augment the ageing Brills, Cuba acquired second-hand electric cars from Spain's Cataluña Railway that had previously been employed in Barcelona suburban service. While decades newer than the original equipment, today even the Barcelona cars have a dated appearance. And a few of the modified older cars soldier on, lending charm to the line.

Although the old Hershey factory shut around 2002, the electric remains a popular tourist attraction and continues to serve the local population. Donncha Cronin visited in 2014, and explained that line is famous for delays, only loosely

Above: A Hershey Electric preserved freight 'motor' (as electric locomotives are properly described) is displayed at the old Hershey station (now called Casa Blanca), which, like the railway itself, took its name from the Pennsylvania-based chocolate confection company.

adhering to its schedule. "This is a journey back in time. It is a life-line to communities along the route. In many places it's difficult to board because there are no platforms, so passengers come in and out through the driver's cab."

At Havana, to reach the electric line's terminal, passengers must cross the bay to Casa Blanca. Cronin related, "you take the ferry from a really run-down waterfront terminal. There's an established check-in procedure before you get on the ferry, owing to a hijacking some years ago. When you get to the far side of the bay, it isn't hard to find the Hershey, you just look to the left and there are the wires! These will lead you to an unromantic station where the staff are moping about all over the place. It reminded me of Casablanca, sans Bogart."

Once on the move the ride is rough. Cronin said, "it's a real seat-of-the-pants journey, but the staff on the car were very personable and enjoyed chatting with passengers." The cars amble along at 6–18 mph (10–30 kph) but the brakes work well (sometimes too well). Much of the countryside isn't well-served by roads, so the electric retains a fair share of local traffic. But since Matanzas is also served by road and faster mainline trains, not many passengers ride the full length of the electric line.

Below: One of the second-hand electric cars from Barcelona pauses on street trackage for its station stop at Casa Blanca. Cuba's Hershey Electric is famous for its laid-back pace of operation and there's a pretty liberal interpretation of the timetable.

CUBAN RAILWAY PRESERVATION
The Survivors

BRIAN SOLOMON

Cuba's reputation as a bastion of railway antiques has fuelled preservation efforts aimed at retaining elements of railway heritage while providing tourist attractions for visitors. The Havana Railway Museum is located in Cristina Station, the old terminal for Ferrocarriles Occidentales de Cuba. This opened in 2009 and houses a variety of antique steam locomotives, most of them built in the United States. One of the prize exhibits in the collection is a locomotive once run by Fidel Castro. Sadly, many of the displays are in poor condition having spent years outdoors without proper restoration. On his visit in summer 2014, Donncha Cronin found that even a visit to the museum was more complicated that expected. "Apparently it isn't always open. I was told that it was 'closed, undergoing restoration'." However, as is often the case in Cuba, with a nod and a wink, and a nominal donation, the museum opened its doors. Elsewhere around

Below: The old Ferrocarriles de Cuba railway terminal is now The Havana Railway Museum, which is undergoing restoration.

Havana, vintage steam locomotives are publicly displayed, notably at the Almacenes San José (Artisans Market).

There are more elusive locomotives to be found on preserved vestiges of steam-powered, sugar-plantation lines. One of the best examples is the tourist train at Trinidad associated with the Valle de los Ingenios plantation. This vast sugar plantation spread over three valleys, largely dating back to the 18th and 19th centuries, is considered one of the best surviving examples of the Caribbean sugar industry. It was listed as a UNESCO World Heritage Centre in 1988 and features 75 structures, many of which have been derelict for decades.

The railway was an integral part of the plantation. An excursion is advertised as working daily, which in theory departs Trinidad at 9.30 a.m. and returns at 2 p.m. However, visitors may wish to inquire in advance as actual operations vary according to demand and the timetable is only loosely interpreted. At Trinidad, a castle-like building appears to have been the original railway terminal, but tickets for the excursion are purchased from a less impressive structure nearby. In addition to the active locomotive, a variety of disused engines are stored on sidings. Passenger cars appear to be adapted from old freight cars and are open-sided.

Donncha Cronin related an adventure on a recent excursion, "at one point the train stopped at a remote place in the middle of nowhere. The train crew

Above: Among exhibits at the Havana Railway Museum are dozens of sugar-plantation steam locomotives as well as more modern engines, such as this Soviet-built M62 diesel electric, which seems massive by comparison.

got off the engine, abandoning the train and its passengers, and chased some goats through a clearing in the village. They singled out a goat and brought it on board and tied it up in the bar car, bleating. Perhaps this was destined to be someone's dinner?" Under ordinary circumstances, the bar served two varieties of beer, 'Crystal', which is a typical lager, and for the more adventurous drinker, 'Bucanero', which features a picture of a pirate.

Left: Havana Railway Museum has become the repository for a variety of antique railway locomotives, many of which are displayed outside. Engine 1904 is a 2-8-0 type built in Wilkes-Barre, Pennsylvania by the Vulcan Locomotive Works and is typical of heavy industrial locomotives of early 20th century America.

Left: A 2-6-0 type steam locomotive number 1593 built by Baldwin in Philadelphia, Pennsylvania, in 1915. This hand-painted engine was up to pressure and assigned to work excursion trains on Cuban's Central Australia plantation railway.

Another vestige of a Cuban sugar-plantation railway is the Central Australia line, located at the remnants of a large plantation factory about half-way between Havana and Santa Clara. Although not listed in many guidebooks, this operation should intrigue the railway enthusiast as it involves an active steam locomotive shed and a two-hour, ambling journey over weed-covered tracks that includes various plantation demonstrations and sometimes a musical interlude performed by the train crew. The related sugar factory was purportedly Fidel Castro's headquarters during the 1961 counter-revolution.

American Travel Advisory

Friction between Cuba and the United States stemming from the 1959 revolution and subsequent events continues to complicate relations between the two nations. As of 2015, US travellers to Cuba should be aware the United States Department of State—Bureau of Consular Affairs website (travel.state.gov) advises that, 'tourist travel to Cuba is prohibited under U.S. law for U.S. citizens and others under U.S. jurisdiction'. However, travel for United States citizens may be authorized for other reasons. Americans planning a visit should investigate the current situation prior to travel.

These pages: An Alco DL-560 diesel-electric leads PeruRail's Andean Explorer across a high plateau in the Andes.

SOUTH OF THE EQUATOR

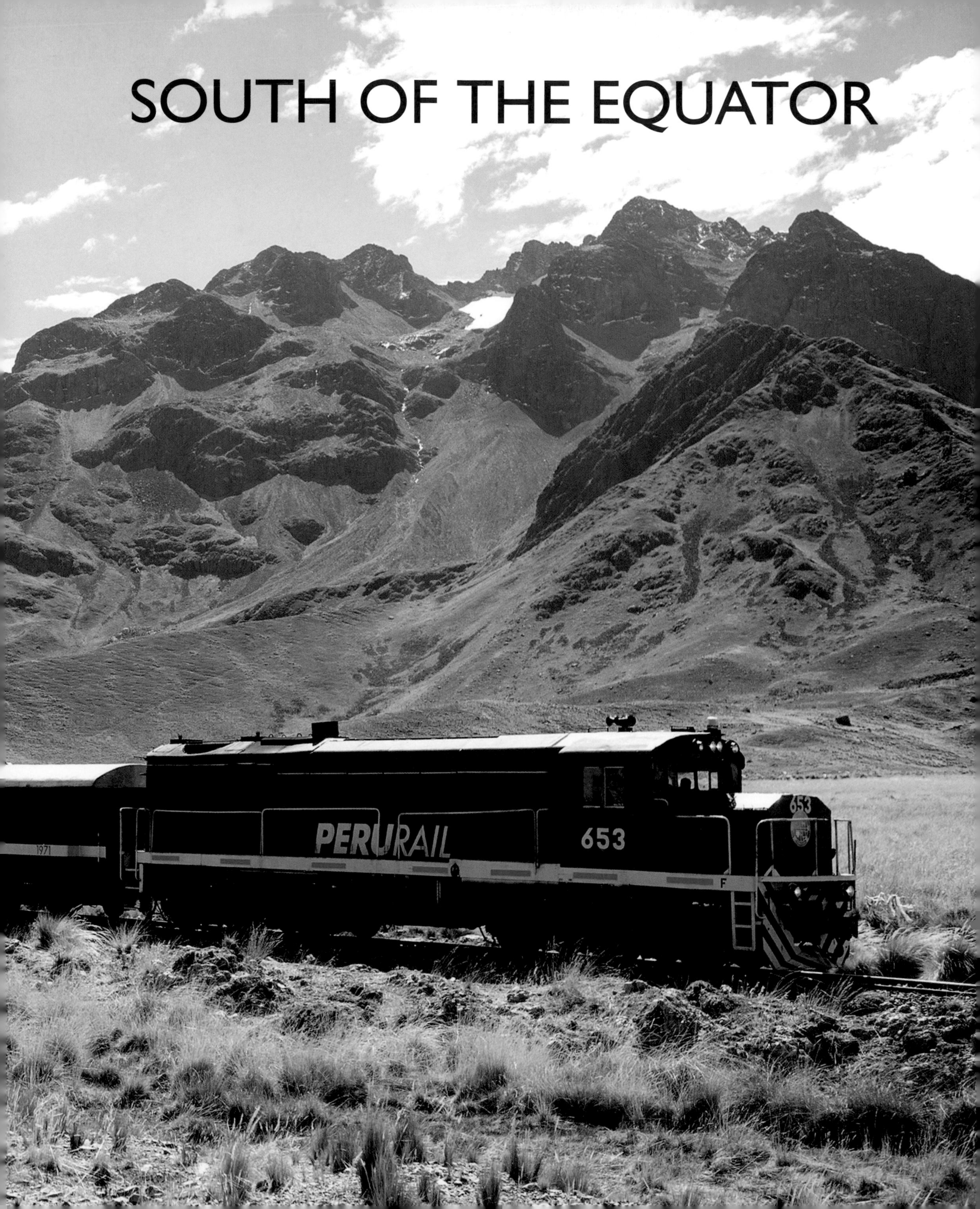

CHILE
TALCA TO CONSTITUCIÓN
A Window on Rural Life

BRIAN SOLOMON

C hile's metre-gauge line from Talca to Constitución is a meandering 55-mile (88-km) route that is one of that country's last active branch passenger railways and offers a lively window on rural Chilean life.

The best way to reach the narrow gauge terminus is by mainline train. Chile's national railway company, Empresa de los Ferrocarriles del Estado (EFE) operates through long-distance passenger services, branded as TerraSur, on its north-south, broad gauge line between Santiago's Alameda Station and the southern city of Chillán. These modern trains connect major points along the line several times daily. EFE's branch trains for the coastal resort of Constitución begin at Talca and operate twice daily, with early morning and evening departures. These use antique German-built railcars (referred to in company literature as Buscarrils ('trainbuses') and represent the antithesis of the modern mainline experience.

Although it's possible to make a cross-platform connection at Talca, where

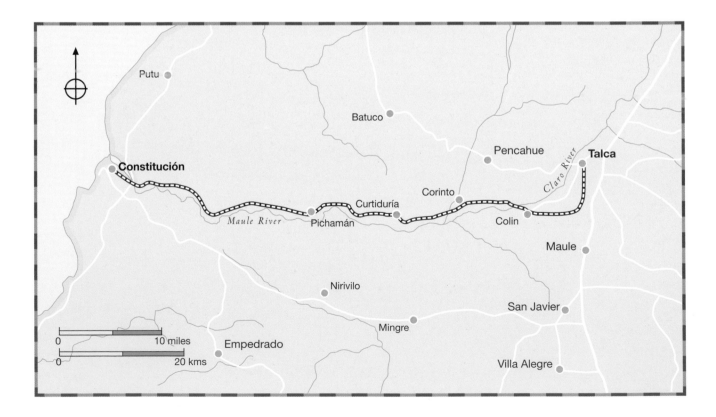

Above: *The calm before the storm: EFE's metre-gauge railcar and centre-door trailer at Talca before its 7.30 a.m. departure to Constitución.*

branch railcars depart from a bay platform, because of the infrequency of normally scheduled branch trains, the best means for visitors to experience the line is by staying overnight in Talca. Tickets for the branch train can be purchased from the Talca booking office.

Despite the light service, the trains tend to be well patronized. Although the line is popular with intrepid tourists, most travellers are locals because roads along the line are few or non-existent. An early arrival is necessary to secure a seat, and the best view is from behind the driver towards the front of the car. It is common for the railcar to tow an unpowered trailer to allow for more passenger accommodation. The ride typically takes 3½ to 4 hours, as the train has many scheduled stops as well as collecting and dropping off passengers at almost any place they desire to go.

The line follows river valleys, first crossing the Claro River west of Colin, about 7 miles (12 km) from Talca. About 19 miles (30 km) from Talca it joins the Maule River Valley and stays near the river for the remainder of the run. The Talca end of the line is characterized by open landscape and vineyards, while further west the scenery closes in and is more rugged, with some remarkable engineering between Pichamán and Constitución. Among the features of the line is a lone tunnel at Quebrada Honda and a spectacular bridge designed by Gustave Eiffel over the Maule near the west end of the line.

At one time this narrow gauge railway was much busier and handled heavy freight as well as passenger trains. However, the loss of its primary freight shipper in 1996 has resulted in scaled-back operations. At many stations there's evidence of disused passing sidings and spurs. The only regularly used siding is at the midway point, formerly known as Infiernillo (Little Hell), but renamed to honour Chilean poet, Jorge Gonzáles Bastías. The schedule shows that both morning and evening trains are due to meet here, and with both trains given the same time, this implies a degree of anticipated punctuality that often exceeds actual operations.

Although Chile is generally known for its dry climate, the centre of the country can suffer from violent rain storms which can affect operations. The Constitución region has also suffered from earthquakes and tsunamis over the years. On the mid-August day Michael Walsh rode the line, fallen trees and rock falls delayed progress on several occasions. In addition to the pair of scheduled trains, EFE occasionally operate extra services to suit the needs of the local population.

Below: The scene from the cab of Talca-Constitución between Toconey and Pichamán finds track workers clearing fallen trees that had blocked the line. The delayed service from Constitución can be seen beyond the trees, and it subsequently reversed back to Pichamán.

Above: *The 7.30 a.m. railcar and trailer from Talca is seen at Constitución reversing from the main platform to turn at a reversing triangle about 650 feet (200 m) to the rear. Storms had brought hours of intense rain, which covered the platforms with water to above rail level.*

Left: *After the storm; two railcars running back to back arrive at Talca in watery sunlight.*

PERU
LAKE TITICACA AND THE
ROUTE OF THE *ANDEAN EXPLORER*
Puno to Cusco

BRIAN SOLOMON

The surface of Lake Titicaca is 12,497 feet (3,809 m) above sea level, making it the world's highest lake and the highest navigable body. It is unusually deep (estimated depth, 1,214 feet/370 m) and covers more than 3,100 sq miles (more than 8,000 sq km). It serves as part of the border between Peru and Bolivia. Historically, the railways of these countries maintained freight interchange using car floats across the lake, while passenger boats connected scheduled railway services. Titicaca's extraordinary elevation is dwarfed by the Andean peaks around it, some of which reach to 21,000 feet (6,400 m) above sea level. Its shores feature ancient settlements, among the oldest in South America.

PeruRail's *Andean Explorer* is one of the finest of several surviving, regularly scheduled railway journeys in a nation famous for nearly mythic railway experiences. It is considered one of the world's great train trips. Typically the *Andean Explorer* runs three to four days per week depending on the season, connecting the town of Puno on Lake Titicaca with Cusco.

Today's train is modern compared with those that plied the line up until a few years ago. It emulates a European-style, Pullman luxury train complete with bar car, observation lounge and diner. This caters for upmarket travellers and is far more expensive than the traditional service that ran the route. The train departs Puno northbound at 8 a.m. with a scheduled 6 p.m. arrival at Cusco. The vistas from the train are extraordinary, featuring an open Andean landscape with a vast sweep of mountain peaks to either side. The entire journey is at high altitude, one of the highest railway journeys in the world.

Above: *The view from PeruRail's* Andean Explorer.

TRAINS TO MACHU PICCHU
From Cusco to the Famous Inca Ruins

BRIAN SOLOMON

Cusco is a terrific town. It is picturesque and features a blend of Spanish and Incan architecture. While the line from Puno used by the *Andean Explorer* is standard gauge (4 feet 8½ inches/1,435 mm), the route running north from Cusco dropping down to the semi-tropical forests is narrow gauge — just under three feet (914 mm). The latter is the primary route to reach the popular tourist attraction of the Incan ruins at Machu Picchu. This makes the route very well travelled — one of the busiest tourist lines in South America.

Machu Picchu was only rediscovered in 1911, when Yale University professor, Hiram Bingham found the isolated site while exploring the Peruvian Andes in search of the legendary city of Vitcos, the last Incan capital. On his way from Ollantaytambo he followed a recently built Peruvian government trail into what he described in National Geographic as a 'wonderful canyon. So lofty are the peaks on either side that although the trail was frequently shadowed by dense tropical jungle, many of the mountains were capped with snow.' He goes on to recognize that the construction of this trail had allowed him to reach this extraordinary canyon and, with the aid of a guide, to find the ruins of Machu Picchu. 'On all sides of us rose the magnificent peaks of the Urubamba canyon, while 2,000 feet below us the rushing waters of the noisy river, making a great turn, defended

Left: Travel in comfort to Machu Picchu: this view shows PeruRail's dining car on the Hiram Bingham.

three sides of the ridge . . . we found ourselves in the midst of a tropical forest, beneath the shade of whose trees we could make out a maze of ancient walls . . .'

Above: A diesel-electric locomotive leads a PeruRail train working the line between Machu Picchu and Cusco.

The narrow gauge railway to Machu Picchu winds its way northwards from Cusco, dropping several thousand feet into the Urubamba canyon. The line follows the Urubamba River and actually goes around the ruins at a much lower level. Although there are glimpses of the Incan city from the train, most passengers are collected from the terminus by a bus to reach the site.

To avoid a series of switchbacks, the present narrow gauge railway station serving Cusco is actually located at Poroy, about 8 miles (13 km) to the west. Travellers recommend reaching the station by taxi or bus. Most trains take three hours 15 minutes to reach Machu Picchu from Poroy, however, there are several trains closer to the Incan ruins that involve shorter journeys. For example, the train ride from Ollantaytambo to Machu Picchu takes less than an hour and a half.

The popularity of this journey offers travellers a host of options since two companies operate trains on the line. PeruRail offers three service grades from Poroy, with its luxurious *Hiram Bingham* being the most expensive and includes on-board entertainment and a guided tour. Its other services are advertised as *Expedition* and *Vista Dome*, and also provide a stop at Ollantaytambo. Inca Rail operates a modern train three times daily from Ollantaytambo.

BOLIVIA
POTOSÍ TO SUCRE
Ringed by Andean Peaks

BRIAN SOLOMON

When it comes to exotic railways, there's no place more exotic than Bolivia, in the opinion of Michael Walsh who has shared his experiences of the country.

Bolivia features a dichotomous railway network. Owing to the nation's difficult terrain and sparsely populated countryside, there is no physical connection between lines in the east and those in the west of the country. For the visitor, the sinuous lines in the mountainous west are of the greatest interest. These are unquestionably some of the most spectacularly scenic in South America.

Historically, Bolivia was the land of the Incas and had been enjoying a highly

developed civilization by the 16th century, at the time of the Spanish invasion and subsequent colonization. Two centuries of Spanish rule effectively enslaved the indigenous population, and by the early 18th century, South American nations fought for their independence. Bolivia is named in honour of Simón Bolívar, a hero of South American liberation.

Modern Bolivia is landlocked; bordered by Brazil to the north and east, Paraguay, Argentina and Chile to the south, and Peru in the west. It is divided into three geographical regions with an estimated three-fifths consisting of the low-altitude Oriente (eastern) region. The central mountain valley region and the eastern Altiplano (high plateau) feature the most impressive scenery, with the majority of the population living in its high-altitude, eastern cities. Volcanic Andean peaks tower up to 21,000 feet (6,400 m) above sea level with key mountain passes above 13,000 feet (4,000 m), placing it among the world's highest inhabited nations. Paradoxically, Bolivia's population has preferred higher regions, a condition attributed to fear of disease and pestilence in the damp eastern lowlands. Mines in the Altiplano have provided employment, and the comparative proximity of mineral riches to Pacific coastal ports in Peru and Chile have contributed to the development of its western railway network.

Below: Some journeys in Bolivia are more adventurous than others. But if nothing unusual ever happened, what stories would you tell?

Overleaf: Empressa Ferroviaria Andina operates a railbus (Bus Carril) on its lightly travelled line between Potosí and Sucre.

Despite mineral wealth, through the mid-20th century Bolivia remained one of the poorest South American nations with its population suffering from an abnormally short lifespan, and it remains exceptionally impoverished. In the mid-1960s, Bolivia was the setting for a Socialist revolution led by Ché Guevara who was killed here in October 1967.

The extraordinarily scenic railway line from Potosí to Sucre connects the historic silver mining area of Potosí with Bolivia's colonial-era capital. Potosí is one of the world's highest cities, located on an open Andean plateau more than 13,700 feet (4,175 m) above sea level. It thrived during Spanish colonial times as the region's mines enriched the city. In its heyday during the mid 17th century, its population exceeded 160,000, which then declined to a fraction of that by the time of Bolivian independence in 1825. In the last 50 years, the city has grown again and is now approaching its former population figures.

Bolivia's Andean railway, Empressa Ferroviaria Andina (FCA), operates a scheduled tri-weekly passenger service using a modern railbus, which departs Potosí at 8 a.m. on Tuesdays, Thursdays and Saturdays, returning Mondays, Wednesdays and Fridays. This takes six hours to travel 107 miles (172 km) with the ride progressing at a leisurely amble. While a line continues west from Potosí to a junction at Rio Mulatos with FCA's north-south line (running from Villazón via Uyuni to Guaqui, covered below), there is currently no regular passenger service.

Potosí station is a large structure built in a handsome railway tradition. Nearby is a largely disused locomotive shed. Potosí is ringed by Andean peaks and there are stunning views in every direction as the line undulates across the high plateau. Patches of fertility break up the landscape characterized by vast barren mountainsides. The railway follows the descent of the mountains from the Altiplano and the terrain is unforgettable; here the railway was expertly fitted into an inhospitable landscape. Although villages dot the landscape, the train makes relatively few stops. However, local people use the train to reach places that are inaccessible by road which makes the ride especially intriguing; how many inhabited places in the world remain beyond the reach of the omnipresent paved roadway?

In a stunning valley approximately 8,530 feet (2,600 m) above sea level, Sucre was established in the 16th century on the site of an existing village, and is known as the City of Four Names, having previously been called Charcas, Chuquisaca and La Plata. It owes much of its modern prosperity to the railway that enabled it to develop as a regional industrial centre. The railway presently terminates at El Tajar, a suburb of Sucre, and train schedules note that service is suspended on the final two miles (three kilometres) to Sucre itself. Michael Walsh commented, 'on the whole Bolivians are friendly, helpful people' but suggested that travellers should exercise caution, especially in cities.

ORURO-UYUNI-VILLAZÓN
To the Argentine Frontier

BRIAN SOLOMON

Western Bolivia is bisected by a north-south Empresa Ferroviaria Andina (FCA) route running from the Peruvian frontier at Lake Titicaca near Guaqui via El Alto (near La Paz), Oruro, Rio Mulatos and Uyuni south to Villazón on the Argentinean frontier (see map on page 122). It is one of the most stunning mountain journeys in the world.

As of 2015, FCA schedules indicated that the complete all-rail journey from Guaqui to Villazón wasn't possible owing to a suspension of service on the line between Oruro and El Alto. A tourist service was available from El Alto and Guaqui. FCA's regularly scheduled trains between Oruro and Villazón include its *El tren Wara Wara de Sur*, and the faster, limited stops *Expreso del Sur*, both of which were on a bi-weekly schedule in 2015.

In recent years, Uyuni has become a favoured location to begin or end a journey on this superbly scenic route. This is a junction on the north-south route where a line from Uyuni to the Chilean frontier at Ollagüe continues to the west (which only has passenger service to Abaroa but not across the border); however, the main attraction is its famous steam locomotive graveyard where dozens of locomotives lie rusting in a stunning Andean setting.

Even for through rail travellers, a layover at Uyuni to see the locomotives should be on the agenda, though the town isn't the nicest place: its well-worn environment is typical of remote South American settlements. The station is relatively small, but has a photogenic setting, although schedules presently show through trains passing southbound at night.

El tren Wara Wara de Sur's southbound schedule tends to get it to Atocha around sunrise, which gives passengers a good opportunity to enjoy one the most scenic portions of the line in daylight. Atocha is 56 miles (90 km) south of Uyuni; this mining town along a windswept river resembles a classic mining camp on the old Colorado narrow gauge as it might have appeared 70 to 100 years ago.

Above: The Uyuni steam locomotive graveyard has been a favourite attraction for railway enthusiasts. Here lie the vestiges of locomotives that once worked the line. Today, diesel-electric locomotives haul most trains, though in the mid-1990s the railroad reactivated a few steam locomotives to meet traffic demands.

South of Atocha is the real attraction: here the line drops through a spectacular mountain valley, featuring vertiginous scenery and odd pinnacles of eroded rock with cacti, where llamas can be seen clinging to the hillside.

Tupiza is the next important stop, two-and-a-half to three hours south of Atocha. This is a pleasant remote mountain town that may also warrant a stop-over.

The terminus is at Villazón, about 11,309 feet (3,447 m) above sea level. The railway once continued across the frontier to the Argentine town of La Quiaca. While conceptually it is walking distance from the Argentinean border, the exceptional altitude can make even a short walk difficult, so it's best to take it easy.

El tren Wara Wara de Sur offers three classes of travel: executive, first and standard, while *Expreso del Sur* has just the top two classes. Trains are led by Japanese-built diesels and, in season, passenger consists tend to be long, as this is a popular journey.

Below: South of Atocha, the railway negotiates some exceptionally rugged scenery on its winding 60-mile (96-km) journey to Tupiza.

ECUADOR
ADVENTURES ON THE GUAYAQUIL-QUITO LINE
Exceptional Engineering

BRIAN SOLOMON

Ecuador encompasses a land area just over 106,000 sq miles (274,545 sq km). Its mainland straddles the spine of the Andes and is bisected east-west by the mid-globe circumferential intersection from which it derives its name. Ecuador built relatively few railways for its size, in part of because of its vertiginous terrain and its largely rural population. In consequence of the former, its primary network is defined by one of the world's most difficult and scenic railway lines. This 3 foot 6 inch (1,067 mm) gauge line runs 452 km (281 miles) from the coastal port at Guayaquil to the inland capital at Quito. Connecting lines include a branch extending south from Sibambe to Azogues and Cuenca, and a route running north/ north-west 373 km (232 miles) from Quito to the coastal port of San Lorenzo.

The mainline is famous for its exceptional engineering. In the early years of the 20th century, the railway was carved into improbable places at extraordinary altitudes. It is best known for its switchback (a zigzag arrangement wherein the train noses into a stub-end then reverses on an adjacent line to gain elevation quickly in tight situations where through construction is impractical) up the face of the Andean ridge called Nariz del Diablo (the Devil's Nose). Here the gradients reach a staggering 5.5 per cent, which test the limits of wheel-rail adhesion. At Palmira (103 miles/166 km from the Guayaquil terminal at Durán) the line crests a summit 10,624 feet (3,238 m) above sea level, and for many miles the line remains above 8,000 feet (2,500 m), putting this among the world's highest railways. It further climbs to a high summit at Urbina, 11,840 feet (3,609 m) above sea level.

During the 1980s and early 1990s, Ecuador railways suffered from unfavourable events. In 1983 portions of the Guayaquil-Quito mainline were washed out, suspending through services. Other lines were closed or scaled back due to economic circumstances. Now, though, Ecuador is a bright spot among South American railways. On a continent where many lines have been closed and abandoned in recent decades, Ecuador has reversed the trend. Recent investment has reopened routes while establishing a number of regularly scheduled tourist trains on key portions of the railway. Ferrocarriles del Ecuador (Ecuadorian Railways Company) boasts in its mission statement that it hopes to, 'effectively manage

ZIMBABWE
VICTORIA FALLS
STEAM TRAIN COMPANY
A Journey Like No Other

DAVID BOWDEN

Steam train enthusiasts who visit the mighty 'Musi-oa-Tunya' or 'Smoke that Thunders' (as the locals call Victoria Falls) need a vivid imagination to conceptualize what was once a mighty rail network. The spectacular falls still lure travellers but these days, they mostly arrive into the recently upgraded Victoria Falls International Airport. While trains operated by National Railways of Zimbabwe still run to Bulawayo and on to Harare, they are slow and often late.

In the early days, guests who travelled to the Falls chose to stay in the Victoria Falls Hotel. Initially, this was a simple structure but it is now one of the most majestic hotels in the whole of Africa with uninterrupted views of the Victoria Falls Bridge. The National Railways of Zimbabwe still has some ownership of the hotel and it is therefore an essential place for rail enthusiasts to visit, dine at or stay in. Stanley's Terrace here has uninterrupted views of the rail and road bridge

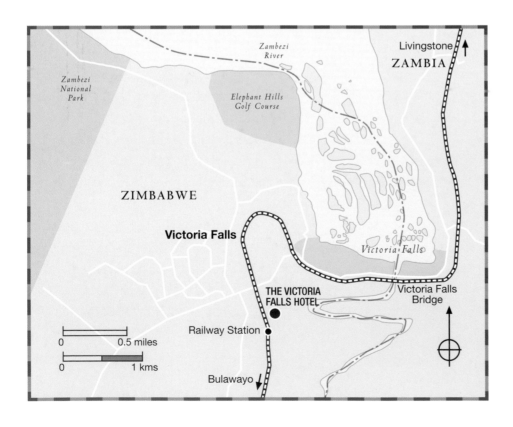

across the Zambezi River leading to Livingstone in Zambia. Guests at the Victoria Falls Hotel were once carried by porters and then via a trolley to the Falls. Started in 1920, the service was eventually disbanded in 1957, although there are plans afoot to reinstate it.

The original railway line ran immediately in front of the terrace but was relocated to the front of the hotel in 1909 after being washed away in a flash flood. Victoria Falls railway station is located within metres of the grand entrance and it is here that the daily overnight train from Bulawayo arrives at the end of its 293-mile (472-km) journey.

In days gone by, travelling by rail to see the 355-foot (108-m) high falls cascade down the Zambezi River was one of the great adventures that attracted inquisitive souls with sufficient funds to travel to such isolated places, then known as Southern Rhodesia (now Zimbabwe). The railway reached the Falls in 1904 and, over time, the *Pride of Africa* train became one of the most exhilarating rail odysseys in the world. Victoria Falls was an essential stop on the rail line that was planned to operate from Cape Town to Cairo (a plan that was never executed). The *Pride of Africa* still runs, operated by Rovos Rail, which runs a four-day, three-night service that starts in Pretoria and travels through Botswana and Hwange

Above: The highlight of the train journeys offered is to pass over and stop on the famous Victoria Falls Bridge between Zimbabwe and Zambia to view the broad expanse of the majestic Victoria Falls.

National Park in Zimbabwe before reaching Victoria Falls on day four. The journey can also be travelled in the opposite direction. Another 14-day excursion, which starts in Cape Town and finishes in Dar-es-Salaam in Tanzania, also makes a stop at Victoria Falls.

The Victoria Falls Steam Train Company

Based at the Victoria Falls station, the Victoria Falls Steam Train Company operates a variety of tourist train trips. Using steam train number 512 and five partly restored heritage carriages, it has an arrangement with the National Railways of Zimbabwe and Zambia Railways to carry passengers across the Victoria Falls Bridge and into Zambezi National Park. This journey partially replicates a journey that started in 1910 and operated every weekend for many years. Known as 'The Weekender', it took passengers from Livingstone in Zambia to Victoria Falls and back.

Train 512 is a Class 14A Garratt, designed and built by Beyer Peacock in Manchester, England, in 1953. It was one of 246 Garratt steam engines that once operated in Zimbabwe. It pulls five carriages including Baggage Car 264, which still contains the original safe that once kept mail and valuables secure. The carriage has been converted into the Zambezi Lager bar carriage, which is especially

Below: While the interior of the carriages reflect a gracious and bygone era, the train in general needs lots of loving attention.

popular on the Zambezi Lager Party Express. The other carriages are Diner 680, a 24-seater carriage built in Lancashire in 1905; Diner 660, a 40-seater carriage similar to Diner 680 but maintained in its original condition; Lounge 4096, a 37-seater carriage built in Gloucester and operated for third-class passengers but refurbished in 2000 as a grander mode of transportation, and Lounge 4108 which is similar to Lounge 4096 and capable of carrying 43 passengers. These opulent, pre-war rail carriages look like museum pieces left over from an era many have forgotten. Efforts are being made to undertake much-needed renovations on the interior and exterior of all the carriages.

Several services are operated by the company and range from private charters to the popular sunset bridge run. Most journeys head across the Victoria Falls Bridge into the Zambezi National Park in Zambia. All involve some form of refreshments, such as canapés and sparkling wine or Zambezi lager and more substantial dinners. A two-hour sunset bridge run heads across the bridge as the

sun goes down and then into the national park. Passengers are allowed off the train while it is on the bridge or they can simply sit back and relax in the historic carriages. This journey has been recognized as one of the best places in the world to appreciate the civilized tradition of the 'sundowner'.

Above: Train 512 of the Victoria Falls Steam Train Company is a Class 14A Garratt, built by Beyer Peacock in 1953.

The Zambezi Lager Party Express speaks for itself and includes a free flow of one of Zimbabwe's favourite brews. It is said that there is no better place to appreciate an ice-cold Zambezi Lager than on the Victoria Falls Bridge perched above the Zambezi River cascading through the deep gorge below the Falls. African Boma and Moonlight Dinner trips are especially popular with groups as the train does the basic sunset bridge trip but then makes an extended stop in the national park where an elaborate three-course dinner is served under the stars. In winter, when it can get quite chilly in the evening, huge bonfires warm up the dining area or meals are served on the train. Themed dinners with African dancers and entertainers are also on hand for those who charter the train to conduct their own programme.

The nostalgic journeys offered by The Victoria Falls Steam Train Company provide an opportunity to relive an era that was so important for the tourist town of Victoria Falls.

KENYA
MOMBASA TO NAIROBI
Of Lunatics and Lions

BRIAN SOLOMON

Board a train at sunset in the thousand-year-old Indian Ocean port of Mombasa and head west into the darkness on a line known for its literary associations with lunatics and man-eating lions.

Nairobi, the capital, was born in the late 19th century as a railway centre. Nicholas Faith in his book *The World The Railways Made* quotes a Kenyan governor as saying "The railway is the beginning of all history in Kenya. Without it there would be no history in Kenya."

Kenya's most significant railway was built by British colonialists as the Uganda Railway to connect the port of Mombasa with Lake Victoria. It was begun in 1896 and reached as far inland as Nairobi in 1903. Despite serving as a relatively obscure line, it became world famous due to two literary connections attracting attention and visitors for more than a century.

When visionary British planners described their intention to penetrate the

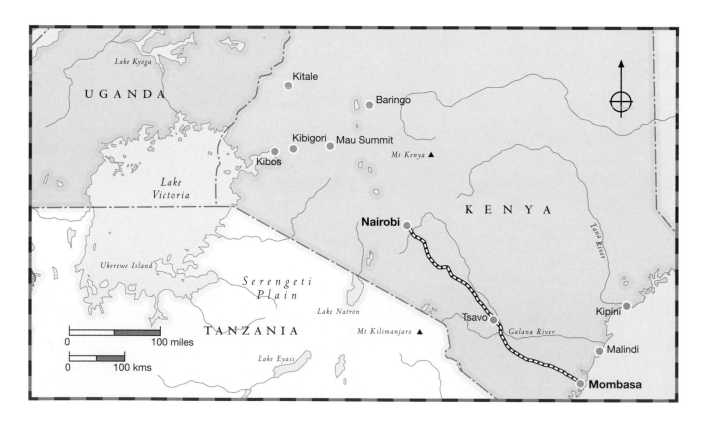

heart of Africa, pushing a railway through rugged, largely unmapped territory populated with wild beasts and malarial mosquitoes, they were perceived as insane by their compatriots in London. Critics of the railway and its promoters dubbed it derogatorily the 'Lunatic Line'. Despite ridicule, not only was the line built, but it also continues to operate today. Yet the name stuck in spite of its success, revived in the 1970s when author Charles Miller titled his popular book on East African colonialism and railway building, *Lunatic Express*. Equally evocative was Colonel J. H. Peterson's 1908 book *The Man-eaters of Tsavo*, which relates the exceptional trials of constructing the line and tells of a pair of lions that devoured no fewer than 28 Indian workers brought in to construct the railway.

Above: Locomotive 2401 of Kenya-Uganda Railway is a 4-8-0 type and one of the displays at the Nairobi Railway Museum. Similar locomotives have been operational for excursion work in recent years.

Despite turmoil and changes to African rail transport, this legendary route remains as one of the few lines in Africa to host a scheduled overnight sleeping car service. From the end of the First World War through much of the mid-20th century, Kenya's railways were operated as part of British colonial East African Railways (EAR), serving Kenya, Tanzania (known as Tanganyika prior to combining with Zanzibar) and Uganda.

In 1977, EAR was dissolved and Kenyan Railways took over. Unfortunately this regime oversaw a general decrease in passenger services, so the run from Mombasa to Nairobi came to symbolize the fading role of European colonial influence in Africa. The old trains, bearing the trappings of elegant travel, including dining-car china, uniformed staff and private sleeping accommodation, became tired, tatty and, in some cases, dangerous. While it was unlikely that passengers would be consumed by lions, fears of thefts aboard trains, and occasional derailments and delays left some travellers dismayed, while others embraced the situation as part of the adventure.

Into the mid-1990s, derelict, British-built, Garratt steam locomotives — of the type that once characterized operations on many African railways — lined sidings and engine terminals along the railway. These dinosaurs of an earlier age had been replaced by diesels, yet like the declining passenger trains, their lingering dereliction appeared emblematic of changes in former African colonies.

Since 2006, Rift Valley Railways (RVR) have operated the historic railway route to Lake Victoria, and in 2013 operated 1,579 miles (2,541 km) of railway lines in Kenya and Uganda. RVR's primary focus has been developing freight traffic on its lines, and today only limited passenger services remain, including Nairobi suburban trains and the famed Mombasa-Nairobi sleeper.

The sleeper makes a 330-mile (530-km) run three nights a week in each direction, departing Mombasa on Tuesdays, Thursdays and Sundays, and Nairobi on Mondays, Wednesdays, and Fridays. Following Victorian British railway practice, the train offers three classes of travel. First and second class are similar providing sleeping-car accommodation, while third class offers a substantially cheaper, coach-only experience. Many western travellers, often solo adventurers and couples, tend to take the first-class accommodation, while third class tends to be the domain of local people.

Mombasa is an ancient port city shaped by more than a millennium of sea trade. It was a toehold for imperial interests and the logical place to build a railway terminal. Today's railway station is just a few dozen feet above sea level. This is a minimal yet functional facility, clearly identified by its English signage.

In 2015, the overnight train to Nairobi was scheduled to depart at 7.00 p.m. Equatorial sunsets occur rapidly, so while the train is boarded at dusk, the light rapidly fades from the sky once the train is underway.

It's an uphill climb away from the Indian Ocean; the line zigzags back and forth as it gently ascends the escarpment above Mombasa. Hurtling into the African night is a thrill as the allure of the unknown is enhanced by darkness. The stories of a lion hunting railway workers in the last century suddenly become more real. Peering into the gloom travellers may catch a glimpse of herds of wild animal in the distance since during the night the line passes through the famed Tsavo safari parks.

It is best to go to the dining car at the earliest opportunity. Beds are made up by staff, and upon returning from the dining car, compartments are prepared for a rolling evening's rest. While actually getting a good night's sleep on board a sleeping car varies from passenger to passenger, the Mombasa-Nairobi train ambles along at a pace that may aid slumber as the train rocks back and forth. If the train grinds to a stop in the middle of the night, it is likely that it's to take a siding to avoid meeting a freight coming the other way. RVR has installed a modern positive train control system using computer and GPS technologies to improve operations and safety.

Sunrise is the highlight of the trip. Depending on the progress of the train overnight, the journey should be more than two-thirds complete by the time the first golden rays illuminate the landscape. Crossing the grassy savannah, passengers may delight in observing giraffes, zebras, ibis, ostrich and other wildlife from the train. On clear days Mt Kilimanjaro looms in the distance.

Nairobi is a great contrast compared with Mombasa. The Kenyan Governor quoted earlier was entirely accurate in regards to Nairobi: before the railway, there was no city here. On the outskirts, the train passes through miles of squalid industrial areas and shantytowns. The city is more than a mile high, and in contrast with its peripheral ugliness, the centre is modern and cosmopolitan punctuated by towering skyscrapers and glass-sheathed modern buildings.

While the cities are vastly different, don't expect a terminal like St Pancras upon arrival at 10 a.m. Although busier than Mombasa's basic station, the Nairobi terminal may be best described as a relic of colonialism. Listen to voices, and you will hear more than a dozen tongues spoken here, both native and European. Nairobi is a centre for tourism, often used as a jumping-off point for safaris.

Among the attractions for the railway enthusiast is the Nairobi Railway Museum. This opened in 1971 under the East African Railway regime and displays a variety of historic equipment, including two surviving Garratt locomotives, one of which has been used for excursions in recent years. It is near the Nairobi station and open most days. Although the railway continues towards the frontier with Uganda, and beyond to Lake Victoria, today these rails are kept polished by the freight trains which make for the larger share of RVR's business.

Below: The Nairobi locomotive shed seen during the steam to diesel transition period. Into the mid-1990s, derelict British-built Garratt steam locomotives could be seen lining sidings in Kenya.

AUSTRALIA
PERTH INTO THE HILLS ON THE HOTHAM VALLEY TOURIST RAILWAY
Western Australia's Only Steam Railway

BRIAN SOLOMON

In the late 19th and early 20th centuries, Western Australia Government Railways (WAGR) developed a network of 3 foot 6 inch (1,067mm) gauge lines extending north, west and south of Perth. The route from East Perth south towards Bunbury opened to Pinjarra in 1883. The branch through the Hotham Valley was extended east from Pinjarra reaching Dwellingup in 1910, and was further extended into the Darling Range to Dwarrda over the next dozen years. This branch served a thriving forestry industry that was fed by a network of lightly built narrow gauge timber lines focused on mills around Dwellingup. Forestry in the region declined in the 1950s, and a terrible bush fire in 1961 devastated

Dwellingup, destroying most of the town and ending much of the activity in the area. The branch continued to haul freight on a limited basis until 1984.

In 1974, a home-grown railway preservation effort centred on Dwellingup marked the beginnings of today's Hotham Valley Tourist Railway. Gradually, this organization worked with WAGR to preserve the steeply graded branch east from Pinjarra while collecting a variety of historic steam and diesel locomotives. Since this line had been worked by Type W, mixed-traffic (freight and passenger service), 4-8-2 Mountain types, four of these engines were acquired and preserved by the railway. In addition, significant diesel-electric locomotives are maintained in working order or are undergoing restoration. For those interested in vintage equipment, there are plenty of old machines on display around Dwellingup.

Two principle routes are operated by the Hotham Valley from their base of activity at Dwellingup. The popular Steam Ranger trips run during the Australian winter between May and October; the memories of Dwellingup's devastation and the constant risk of bush fire between November and early May limit the use of steam locomotives during those months, although diesel trains work the line off season. Passenger excursions head west from the Hill Country at Dwellingup and down the gradient dropping towards Pinjarra on the coastal plain, with

Above: Among the prizes of the Hotham Valley Tourist Railway are four Type W 4-8-2 Mountain locomotives, such as number 945 seen in steam. These engines were designed for light-axle-load, branch-line services and built in the early 1950s in England by Beyer-Peacock for the Western Australia Government Railways.

based on local traffic demands, anticipated construction costs and the viewpoints of railway builders and railway engineers who at times have been at odds with each other. Broad gauges were advocated because they offered greater stability, allowed for larger trains (and in theory more carrying capacity) and overcame technical problems in the 19th century relating to locomotive design. Narrow gauge railways offered an economical solution, since they allowed for tighter curvature, required less substantial infrastructure and gradients, and smaller, lighter railway equipment. Around the world, narrow gauge lines have been built in areas where standard gauge lines were deemed cost-prohibitive.

Inevitably gauge differences result in operational problems. Trains built for one track width cannot easily use the tracks of another width. This limits the ability for through operations and produces a variety of complications where lines of different widths interface. To overcome incompatible gauges, through trains can either go through time-consuming, bogie-swapping exercises (where wheel sets of one gauge are exchanged for those of the other), require expensive gauge-changing trains which pass through gauge changing stations at slow speed to adjust the wheels to the appropriate width (as used in Spain), or involve building dual gauge or 'mixed gauge' tracks.

Mixed gauge track is the oldest means of accommodating trains using different gauges on the same line. Historically, the most common type of mixed gauge is three-rail track where one rail is shared. Where the difference in gauge is too tight to allow adequate space for wheel sets between outside rails in the three-rail system, four rail interlace track is used. In both three-rail and four-rail systems, track work becomes especially complex at junctions and in yards and terminals where switches and points must accommodate multiple gauge track.

Although these are a nightmare for railway engineers as they are more expensive to build, design and maintain, mixed gauge tracks are a delight for railway enthusiasts. Since mixed gauge operations result in added complexity and cost, wherever possible railways try to resolve the problem by investing in re-gauging lines to a common standard. Complexity and peculiarity are among the chief qualities that make a railway exotic in the eyes of the discerning enthusiast. So while streamlining makes complete sense from economic and operational standpoints, it makes for a less interesting railway to observe. Most modern railways have simplified gauge problems, and in 2014, mainline mixed gauge operations are very unusual in all but a few places.

Australian Mixed Gauge

Australia's railways have had an unusual history resulting in extensive systems using three different track widths. In addition to the Stephenson standard gauge,

many Australian lines were built to the Irish broad gauge standard (5 foot 3 inches/ 1,600 mm), while others adopted the narrow 3 foot 6 inch (1,067 mm) gauge.

In the late 19th century, Western Australia Government Railways (WAGR) began building a narrow gauge network (see Hotham Valley Tourist Railway, pages 142 to 145). While this network was entirely isolated from the rest of Australia's railways, the gauge difference presented few problems. However, construction of standard gauge lines complicated matters. Although Australia has been trying to resolve the problems of its incongruent gauges since the mid 1940s, examples of multiple gauges remain.

Above: A narrow-gauge electric suburban train at East Guildford. Take special note of the mixed gauge crossovers in the distance. These provide access to the western leg of a triangular junction connecting to a line that diverges to the south.

In the 1960s, a new standard gauge/mixed gauge route in western Australia was built, resulting in a heavily travelled, mixed gauge line running from Perth to Northam for passenger and freight traffic. This was designed to provide a through standard gauge link from the east all the way to Perth on Australia's west coast for the existing standard gauge Trans-Australia Railway, which had previously terminated at a junction with the narrow gauge system at Kalgoorlie. Coincident with this work was a significant project to re-align the existing narrow gauge mainline between Northam and Midland Junction with a new mixed gauge, low grade mainline along the Avon River Valley through the Darling Ranges. The old narrow gauge route via Clackline was abandoned, which had featured long stretches of steep grades up to 1 in 40.

Riding the Mixed Gauge from Perth to Northam

A busy, local, suburban, narrow gauge passenger service provides transport between Perth and Midland. To the east of Midland, the narrow gauge to Northam is largely used for freight, while the standard gauge is used to link up with lines in the east. A sparsely operated standard gauge passenger service continues over the mixed gauge line east of Midland to the end of mixed gauge track at Northam and beyond. These intermediate distance trains are run by Transwa, with some trains running all the way to Kalgoorlie and others terminating west of there. Perth to Northam takes about an hour and a half, while the full run Perth to Kalgoorlie requires six to seven hours.

Transwa uses modern two and three-piece diesel rail cars on this route, larger and heavier than those used on European railways, that offer extremely comfortable accommodation with two-by-two seating. Seats can be turned to face either direction to suit passenger needs.

East of Midland the scenery is pleasant rather than dramatic, but very rural. In the Avon Valley there is light vegetation and bush. From the train you can see kangaroos and listen to a cacophony of wild parrots fluttering in the trees. Wildlife tends to become scarce during the middle of the day and is best observed in the mornings or evenings. The new line required some difficult engineering in order to reduce the gradient, and the modern trains seem to glide along almost effortlessly.

For the track enthusiast, one of the most interesting characteristics of the line is at Midland. Between Perth and Midlands, the north rail is shared by standard and narrow gauge trains to facilitate access to the suburban platforms, but at Midland the narrow gauge switches from the north rail to the south rail using a very unusual, if not completely unique, interline switch. Most passengers are blithely unaware of this peculiarity, but it makes for a rare distinction that places the passenger service here in the realm of the exotic.

Left: Australian mixed gauge features some wonderfully complex trackage, such as this dual-gauge facing crossover between Ashfield and Bassendean stations on the Midland line. Notice how the shared rail changes sides within the crossover. On the section with shared passenger service, the shared rail is the inner rail on both tracks of the double line. Farther east, where there is no shared passenger running, the common rail is the northern rail on both tracks, an arrangement that requires simpler switches.

THE WEST COAST WILDERNESS RAILWAY
The Train that Refuses to Die

DAVID BOWDEN

The West Coast Wilderness Railway operates as a restoration of the original Mount Lyell Mining and Railway Company Limited service from Queenstown to Strahan (Regatta Point) on the far south-west coast of the island of Tasmania. Even today there is very little land between where the steam train operates and the nearest landfall of Antarctica to the south, across the windswept Southern Ocean.

When construction started on the 3 foot 6 inch (1,067 mm) gauge railway in 1895, the area was one of the most remote parts of the world and not much has changed. Despite roads connecting Queenstown and Strahan to civilization, such as Hobart, the state capital, there's still a sense of entering the lost world once the train ventures into the lush temperate forests along the 22-mile (35-km) route.

Discovering copper in Queenstown was one thing; getting the copper concentrate to the port of Strahan and market was another. A route was identified through the mountainous topography of the steep ravines of the King River and the dense rainforest. Some 500 labourers worked in dangerous conditions on the railway that took two and a half years to dissect the forest. The summers were steaming hot and the winters cold and wet. Reports indicate that only two died in the railway's construction and that the authorities appeared surprised the figure was so low. Fettlers and their families lived in makeshift camps to maintain the line once it was built.

Opposite: The scenery along the journey from Queenstown to Regatta Point features wild rivers and untouched forests; the train travels slowly enough for photographers to capture the scenic beauty.

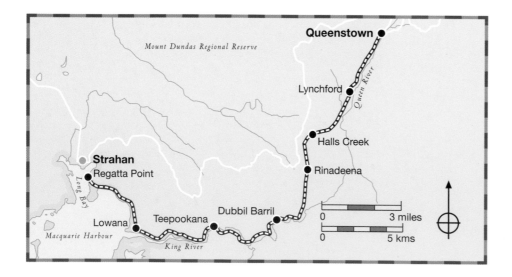

An Abt rack and pinion system was incorporated into sections of the line to enable trains to haul heavy loads up the steep terrain (1:12). Five engines eventually operated on the line and it was one of only two such systems to be established in Australia (the other operated at Mount Morgan in Queensland). The system (with solid bars and vertical teeth) was invented by Swiss engineer, Dr Roman Abt and first used in Harzbahn, Germany in 1885. The teeth in the middle of the rails engaged with a small cogwheel underneath the locomotive to 'drag' it up hills while acting as a brake on the downhill sections.

When the train started service in 1897 it was lauded as a magnificent engineering feat. The railway crossed 60 timber bridges of stepped trestles with the extension from Teepookana to Strahan being completed in 1899. The original railway remained in service for 67 years while the first road only connected Queenstown to the outside world in 1932.

The railway survived floods, bushfires and wash-outs but by 1963 rising maintenance bills forced the mining company to resort to using trucks to transport the copper by road to Strahan. The railway fell into disrepair until 1999 when a restoration proposal was suggested and accepted. Bushfires, floods and natural attrition had further taken their toll and the stations had all disappeared apart from Regatta Point and a section of Queenstown. The five trains were also in various states of disrepair and scattered around Tasmania and the mainland.

Above: The train passes through remote and pristine forests where, on the steep sections, it is assisted by the rack and pinion system situated between the two rails.

After a significant injection of funds, the track and infrastructure were restored and a section of the railway reopened in 2000. The new train features purpose-built carriages fitted out with Tasmanian timbers and modelled on the original Mount Lyell carriages. After a three-year restoration programme, the full service from Queenstown to Strahan was reintroduced in December 2003.

The tourist train departs from Queenstown in the morning and follows the Queen River before reaching Halls Creek Siding where the rack and pinion system is engaged. The section from Halls Creek to Rinadeena Saddle attains gradients of 1:16 or 6.2 per cent and passengers soon appreciate the importance of the Abt system. Just prior to reaching Dubbil Barril and the end of the rack and pinion system, the train passes the picturesque King River Gorge. The route closely follows the river down to Lowana where the King River meets the vast Macquarie Harbour. Now on flat ground, the line heads north all the way to Regatta Point on the outskirts of the coastal village of Strahan.

Passengers have three journeys from which to choose: the Rack and Gorge (Queenstown – Dubbil Barril – Queenstown), the River and Rainforest (Strahan – Dubbil Barril – Strahan) or the Queenstown Explorer (Strahan – Queenstown – Strahan). The first two are half-day journeys while the last is a full-day experience. Two types of tickets are sold with a standard fare in a Heritage Carriage or a higher fare in a Wilderness Carriage which includes a glass of Tasmanian sparkling wine for which the state is famous, transfer to a balcony carriage, morning tea, lunch or afternoon tea (depending upon the route).

Passengers departing from Queenstown can enjoy refreshments in the Tracks Café before departure, browse through the Railway Gift Shop for train literature and excellent Tasmanian produce or learn more about the train in the Abt Railway Museum. Activities such as gold panning, honey tasting, a rainforest walk and wine tasting add to the journey's excitement. Fine Tasmanian table wines such as Pinot Noirs and Sauvignon Blancs are offered along with the sparkling wine. Tasting Tasmania's unique leatherwood honey from hives located in the Teepookana Plateau rainforests is another highlight.

There are six stops along the journey: Lynchford, Halls Creek, Rinadeena, Dubbil Barril, Lower Landing/ Teepookana and Lowana. One of the most scenic sections is through the 500-foot (163-m) deep King River Gorge where the train passes along an embankment 200 feet (65 m) above the wilderness river rushing below.

Three Abt steam trains are used from Queenstown and include Abt 1 dating back to 1896, Abt 3 (1898) and Abt 5 (1938) with the first two considered to be the world's oldest fully-restored working locomotives. The

Below: The train crosses over 60 stepped trestle bridges that have been admired as great engineering feats.

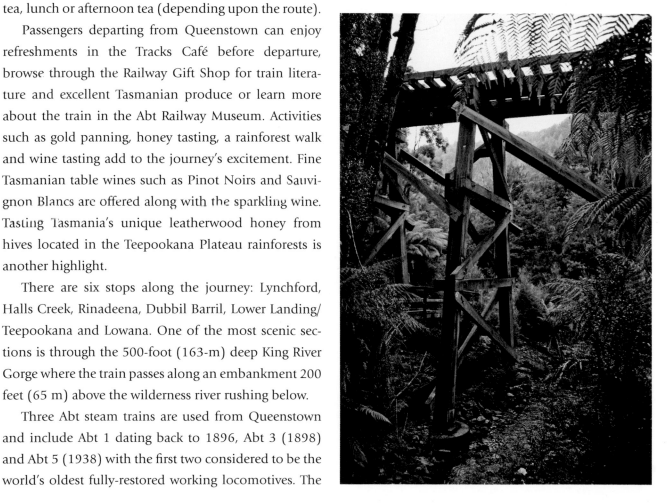

railway also operates two original Mount Lyell Drewry 0-6-0 diesel locomotives on the latter section of the track. Regatta Point is a short distance from the village known best as the departure point for boat cruises on Macquarie Harbour and the UNESCO World Heritage Site of the Gordon River.

There are no longer passenger trains on the small Australian island of Tasmania but there are other trains and museums to explore – Wee Georgie Wood, Redwater Creek Steam and Heritage Society, Don River Railway, Derwent Valley Railway, Launceston Tramway Museum, Tasmanian Transport Museum, Railtrack Riders and Ida Bay Railway. Now revitalized as a tourist train, the West Coast Wilderness Railway is one steam train that simply refuses to die.

Left: The final stretch of the line skirts the coast before reaching the terminal at Regatta Point near Strahan.

Above: *A steam locomotive hauls the carriages of the West Coast Wilderness Railway for the first half of the journey.*

Left: *An original Mount Lyell Drewry 0-6-0 diesel locomotive is coupled to the train for the final section of the track into Regatta Point.*

THE GHAN
A Journey to the Red Centre and Beyond

DAVID BOWDEN

The majority of Australia's 23.13 million citizens live near the coastline of the vast continent. The heaviest concentration is around the south-east from Sydney to Melbourne; beyond the fertile coast, there's not much

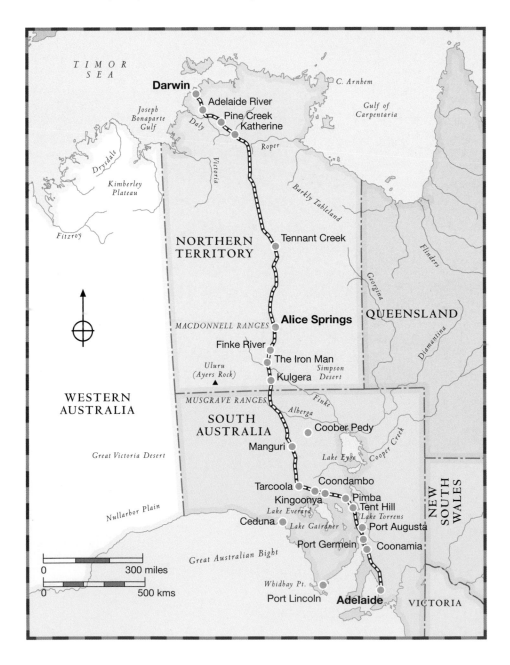

civilization in what is known to most as The Outback. Head further inland and the Red Centre with its dramatic but parched landscapes and skies laden with stars provides a moonscape like nothing else on earth.

Above: Parts of Central Australia, especially around the MacDonnell Ranges along the route of The Ghan, are renowned for brilliant, rich colours, which contribute to the area being called the Red Centre.

Access has never been easy and communications just as difficult. The Overland Telegraph Line, extending 1,988 miles (3,200 km) from Darwin (Northern Territory) to Port Augusta (South Australia), brought Australia into the 19th century and into contact with the rest of the world when it opened in 1872. Camels and camel drivers from Afghanistan (and several neighbouring countries) were brought to Australia to bring in provisions for the line's construction along the desolate and treacherous route.

Cameleers and their camels were also on hand in 1878 to assist with the construction of the railway line north from Port Augusta. However, it wasn't until 1929 that Adelaide was linked by railway to Alice Springs. Volumes have been written about the long and protracted journey that the railway has taken.

In 1883, an ambitious North Australia Railway forged southwards from Palmerston (Darwin) with the long-term vision of linking with the line heading north from South Australia. The southern line eventually reached and stopped in Alice Springs while the line tracking down from the north only reached and provided access to places such as Adelaide River, Palmerston, Pine Creek and Katherine but wasn't connected to Alice Springs in the south until many decades later.

Both were narrow gauge lines of 3 foot 6 inches (1,067 mm) but this was progressively changed in the south starting in 1957 with a standard 4 foot 8½ inches (1,435 mm) gauge. The standard gauge was extended through to Alice Springs in 1980 but it wasn't until January 2004 that the line eventually connected Alice Springs to Darwin in the north. Known as the Central Australian Railway, operations officially started in August 1929. This came to be known as the Afghan Express, which in turn was abbreviated to *The Ghan*, the name which has stuck.

Steam trains ceased operating to Alice Springs in 1951 when they were replaced by diesel-electric locomotives. Because the steam locomotives needed water, the original route was carefully plotted to pass remote and desert locations where precious water could be sourced from artesian bores. When the new line opened in 1980 for diesel locomotive use, the need for water was no longer paramount and the new track was installed 100 miles (160 km) to the west of the original route.

The Ghan, operated by Great Southern Railway, runs from Darwin to Adelaide. The standard one-way trip lasts three days and two nights (54 hours) with a new four-day, three-night journey having just been introduced on services from late May to late August on the Darwin to Adelaide route only.

Most passengers are amazed at the length of the 30-carriage train which normally measures 2,329 feet (710 m) inclusive of two diesels (National Pacific NR Class locomotives along with AN and DL Classes), guest and crew carriages, restaurants, bars, power van and car-transporter carriages. It operates at an average speed of 53 mph (85 kph) and a maximum of 71 mph (115 kph). On each journey, it consumes 10,560 gallons (40,000 litres) of diesel fuel and each carriage carries 793 gallons (3,000 litres) of water. Thirty crew serve the Platinum, Gold and Red Class passengers housed in accommodation ranging from luxurious cabins to reclining seats.

Platinum passengers enjoy large private cabins, lounge seating (that converts to a double bed in the evening), en suite bathroom and all meals of regionally-sourced produce and beverages including excellent Australian wines. The facilities are similar for those in Gold Class but with less lavish and less spacious accommodation. Both classes share the Outback Explorer Lounge and the Queen Anne Restaurant. Red Class passengers are provided with reclining seats and meals in Matilda Café.

Despite passing through desert for much of the journey, the dramatic and ancient Australian landscape is ever-changing. Stops and complementary off-train excursions are conducted at Katherine and Alice Springs with the quirky underground opal mining settlement of Coober Pedy being a new destination on the four-day journey. Passengers on the standard southern journey board the train on Wednesday morning and pass through the lush Top End before arriving in

Katherine after lunch. Here, passengers can visit Nitmiluk Gorge and cruise on the picturesque Katherine River before a late afternoon departure (from late May to late August, there is an additional departure from Darwin only on Saturday and in December and January, there is one departure every fortnight).

After a journey of 882 miles (1,420 km), *The Ghan* arrives into Alice Springs situated in the majestic MacDonnell Ranges just after breakfast on day two. After visiting the local sights, passengers re-board for a departure in the early afternoon for the final 969 miles (1,559 km). In the evening, the train stops at Manguri near Coober Pedy for an outback evening under the dazzling stars in a clear desert night. Adelaide is the final destination on day three with the train arriving into the South Australia capital just before noon.

While the train is air-conditioned, there are several side trips from the train and getting the season right is important. Two seasons dominate central and northern Australia: the dry season (May to October) and the wet season (November to April). The dry season is the most popular time to visit because the weather is cooler, humidity lower and there is usually no rain. In the wet season, monsoonal rains may cut roads and close access to some off-train venues.

Great Southern Railway also operates two other iconic Australian rail journeys – the *Indian Pacific* (Perth to Sydney) and *The Overland Train* (Melbourne to Adelaide). While possibly overshadowed by Australia's equally famous train, the *Indian Pacific*, *The Ghan* remains one of the world's great train journeys and an Australian national treasure.

These pages: Porto's modern tram network opened in 2002. One line crosses the Douro River on the Ponte Luis I, the enormous bridge designed by Gustav Eiffel.

ON THE EDGE OF EUROPE

UKRAINE
BUDAPEST TO UKRAINE AND BACK
A Foray by Rail Across a Forgotten Empire

BRIAN SOLOMON

I t was July, and suitably hot when Denis McCabe and I flew from Dublin to Budapest with the aim of working our way east by train. It is possible to explore central Europe by train but not in one single journey. You can plan a route in advance, or you could opt for a series of spontaneous journeys as we did. Starting at Budapest's Keleti Station, we bought first-class tickets for the *Pannonia* destined for central Romania. Curiously, although the MÁV (Hungarian Railways) office was equipped with computers, international tickets were filled out by hand: a laborious process, but ticket-buying was easier here than further east.

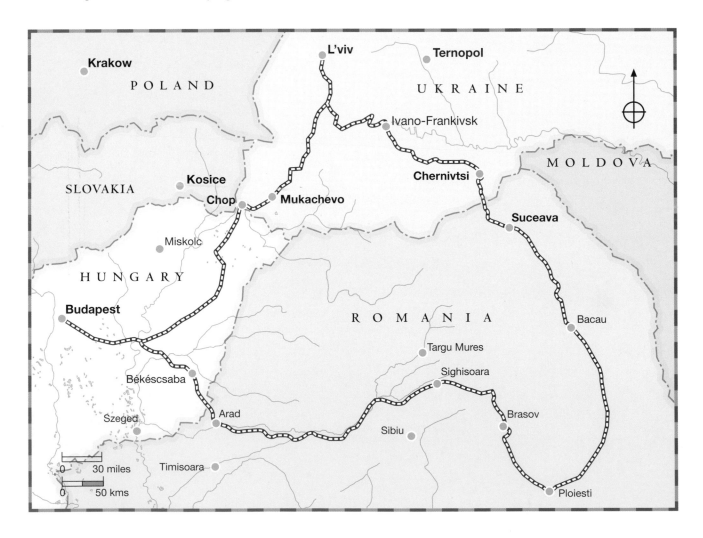

Soon we were ensconced in our compartment on the train beneath Keleti's impressive 19th-century shed. First class on the *Pannonia*, while adequate, was by no means plush. Our train pulled out just after 8.30 a.m., and I watched from the windows as railway security men in black shirts and fluorescent yellow vests were evicting some of Budapest's less fortunate residents from station benches.

Above: A view at dusk looking down Budapest Keleti's iconic, fan-shaped, front window reveals the tracks beneath the shed that lead to myriad destinations across the now-defunct Hapsburg Empire.

The journey crosses the Hungarian plain to Békéscsaba, near the border with Romania, where the *Pannonia* makes a prolonged stop as heaps of belongings on the platform are loaded onto the train by local people. The MÁV car doesn't continue across the border so passengers need to move from the MÁV first-class carriage to a slightly less salubrious CFR (Romanian Railways) first-class carriage. A little while later the Hungarian-Romania frontier is crossed at Lököshárza.

One of the fascinating themes to this eastward journey is that less than a century ago the towns and villages would have been part of the now nearly forgotten Hapsburg empire. Austria-Hungary was the big loser in the Great War, after which everything changed. Suddenly, Hungary found that many of its once-important railway lines, having been effectively truncated by the re-drawing of the eastern European map, no longer served much of a useful purpose. The Second World War resulted in more changes: Stalin's Soviet Union changed borders and moved people in ways that effectively altered the dynamics of the old order altogether. The collapse of the Soviet Union and retrenchment of Russian influence have resulted in more changes.

Once on Romanian rails, the condition of the permanent way varied, and in many places we found heavily used but grass-covered rights of way shared by a variety of passenger and freight trains. At Suceava, modern investment has restored the grand old station that still hinted at its Hapsburg lineage. We saw long trains heading for the Ukrainian frontier. That was the direction we were heading, but not speaking Romanian, and with only an out-of-date Thomas Cook timetable and a travel guide we had trouble buying international tickets.

Finally, a kindly woman ticket seller explained with a wink and a nod that we should get our tickets to the Ukraine from the coach attendants. Armed with this knowledge I formed a plan. We learned that a Ukrainian-bound express was due to make a prolonged station stop at Suceava after 1 p.m. Although neither of us spoke Ukrainian either, using the guide book as an aid I wrote out in Cyrillic: Odessa, Kiev and the name of the nearest Ukrainian city to the frontier (spelled in English as either Chenovcy or Chernivtsi).

Above: Around border areas with Ukraine, four-rail interlace tracks are used to accommodate both Russian gauge (5 foot/1,520 mm) and European standard gauge (4 foot 8½ inches/1,435 mm) trains. This track is near the Romanian border on the way from Suceava to Chernivtsi.

The train roared behind red-and-white CFR electrics and squealed to a halt. There were about 15 heavy Russian passenger carriages, so we strategically positioned ourselves near the rear of the train. I approached one of the women car attendants with my list. I pointed to the word Odessa and nodded at the train. "Nyet!"; Kiev? "Nyet!", then finally Chernivtsi, to which she said nothing, but nodded and led us on board.

We'd passed the first hurdle, *now* it was time to negotiate. She directed us to an empty compartment and in a few minutes the train eased out of Suceava. This carriage was antique stuff, harking back to the days of the Soviet Union with its red weave carpet, burgundy vinyl fold-down seats that could double as beds and safety boxes below for valuables. Above was a second tier of beds, as the compartment was designed for four people. The corridors were clad in uniformly brown Formica. Prevailing throughout was a musty smell of old train stock that reminded me of trips on British tourist railways. Progress towards the frontier was very slow. Our attendant came to negotiate our fare. 'Ten euros' she indicated with her fingers. She seemed unsure until I produced a crisp note and the deal was done. An hour or so later we stopped for Romanian customs. Passports were thumped and a very well-dressed official inquired if we had pistols. Luckily, we did not.

At the Ukrainian customs point border guards boarded the train, mostly, it seemed, to chat with the train attendants. However, in addition to customs and passport formalities, the train had to be re-gauged, which involved shunting the entire train into several sections, then jacking up each carriage and sliding out the 4 foot 8½ inch (1,435 mm) gauge bogies and replacing them with those of the Russian 5 foot gauge (1,520 mm), before reassembling the train.

A classic Russian 2M62 diesel took over for the remainder of our journey. It wasn't long before we arrived at Chernivtsi. This was as far as we could travel on this train. As it turned out, it was also a crew change, which was no coincidence — the woman who had arranged our passage was only going this far, and thus we would need to arrange other transport from here. The engine was changed again, and more carriages added to the consist.

Below: After adding a few cars and changing locomotives, the train from Bucharest to Kiev is ready to depart Chernivtsi. In the lead is a common 2M62 two-piece diesel-electric. Although thoroughly Soviet built, the M62 is derived from American technologies.

The next morning we experienced buying tickets Ukrainian-style. There must be a method to the queueing process, but this eluded us. Among the features of queueing are old women who like to skip to the front of the queue, not to buy tickets, but to remonstrate with whoever sits behind the window. I was warned of this in my guidebook and we experienced this event everywhere we went. Some time later, despite queue-jumping grannies, Cyrillic alphabet and language difficulties, and a culture of bureaucracy, we had our first-class tickets for L'viv.

L'viv, L'vov, Lemberg

While not especially fast, Ukrainian trains travel at a steady pace. The tracks are heavily built, well ballasted and provide a smooth ride. Scheduled trains throw out the anchor at stations, and the stops seem much longer than necessary, but we eventually reached the former capital of Austrian Galicia after a pleasant journey through farm country. What was once Lemberg has had its national affiliation changed three times in less than a century. After the First World War it was part of a re-established Polish state, called L'vov (or Lwów). But Second World War-era changes placed it in Soviet Ukraine. Today it is L'viv.

The L'viv railway station is a palace. The city a beautiful place, akin to Prague or other Hapsburg cities in its elaborate architecture, suffering from many worn bricks and dusty cobblestone streets. It is one of most fascinating cities I've ever visited and a wonderful place for railway enthusiasts. Trams navigate along street trackage, while a continual parade of freight and passenger traffic work the mainlines around the city centre.

After a few days in L'viv we travelled on a through train (that had originated in Moscow) over the Carpathians to Mukachevo (or Mukacheve). It's a long journey from the Russian capital, and the other passengers had been riding for days

We spent an evening exploring Mukachevo — another city with a complex history; it had been variously a part of Transylvania and Carpathian Ruthenia, which during the interwar period was part of Czechoslovakia and after the war was incorporated into Soviet Ukraine. On the following day we rode to Chop, near the present three-way border between Ukraine, Slovakia and Hungary. Here we saw lots of dual gauge interlace trackage to accommodate the gauge differences between eastern and western European networks.

We transited Ukrainian immigration/customs at Chop. Copies of the customs forms I filled out on my first day were collected without so much as a word spoken, and soon we were on a one-car international train heading for the Hungarian border. This was then coupled to an intercity express and we headed back to Budapest in style.

Previous page: L'viv is a classic European city that has suffered through a century of trying times. It features Hapsburg-style architecture and a ten-route, metre-gauge tram network. A Tatra model T4SU tram works cobblestone streets at Rynok Square.

Left: The main railway station in L'viv has a magnificent, classic, steel-arched train shed built in the Hapsburg period. A Ukrainian State Railways (UZ) class ChME3 diesel shunting locomotive glides through the shed.

Above: *An electric local train pauses for passengers at Mukachevo. During the interwar period, Mukachevo was part of independent Czechoslovakia, but the USSR moved the border westwards after the Second World War.*

Left: *Many of Ukraine's lines are electrified to Russian standards. Long-distance passenger trains pass each other in L'viv. In the lead on the left is a class ChS4 dual voltage electric locomotive designed for both 3000 volt DC and 25kV AC overhead systems.*

ESTONIA
FORMER SOVIET RAILWAYS IN A NEW ECONOMY
The Legacies of Russian Influence

BRIAN SOLOMON

Estonia is a small Baltic country on the north-eastern edge of Europe. With a landmass only slightly larger than Denmark and a population of just over 1.25 million, Estonia is one of Europe's smallest nations. Historically, it hasn't been a place that many people visit to ride trains, which is a shame. While not as scenic as Switzerland or as remote as Bolivia, it has a fascinating former Soviet railway system that remains largely undocumented, which makes an Estonian railway journey an exotic exercise for the serious railway traveller.

Below: Electric suburban trains bask in the glow of a double rainbow at their Tallinn terminal. Estonian independence from the Soviet Union has enabled the country to flourish, yet it retains many ties to Russia.

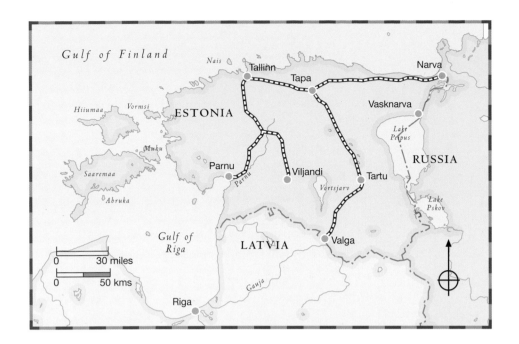

Over the centuries, Estonia was variously dominated by its larger more militant neighbours, including Prussia and Scandinavian countries. However, in modern times, Russia has exerted the greatest influence on the country. Estonia, along with adjacent Baltic states, Latvia and Lithuania, was carved out of the ruins of the Tsarist Russian Empire after the First World War. Independence was brief, and in 1940 it was incorporated into the Soviet Union, where it reluctantly remained a part until regaining independence in 1991.

Estonian Railways

Among the legacies of Russian influence is a large ethnic Russian population (about 30 per cent of the total) and its railway network, most of which was built during periods of Russian/Soviet administration and reflects Russian standards, including its broad (5-foot/1,520-mm) track gauge and large loading gauge. Russia remains Estonian Railways' principal international connection, and provides a large source of freight traffic as well as through long-distance passenger trains.

Although Russia began developing its railways in the 1840s, Estonia only opened its first line in 1870. This route, running from Paldiski via Tallinn to Narva (on the present-day border with Russia), remains one of Estonia's most important lines and is part of the through route to St Petersburg. Estonian broad gauge railways had reached more than 480 miles (770 km) by the time the Soviets reintegrated its system in 1940. Estonia also had a significant narrow gauge network. Although Tallinn had begun electrifying key suburban routes in the 1920s, Estonian railways did not benefit from significant Soviet-era electrification and most

after some nominal modification, including re-gauging, were set up for service on former Soviet rails. I was lucky enough to ride a freight train with Vladimir, the engine driver, from Tallinn to Tapa, part of the route that terminates at Narva. The train had two freshly painted GE C36-7is, yet these still featured Union Pacific seats with that railroad's classic emblem on them.

Eesti Raudtee is a major carrier of Russian produce, primarily semi-refined crude oil brought from Russia. On the return journey back to the Russian frontier at Narva the train consists entirely of empty oil wagons. Accelerating up to track speed on the mainline east of Tallinn didn't strain the pair of American giants. Not only were these more powerful than their Russian counterparts, but they also required far less maintenance. Not everyone on the railway was happy about this. In the shop, a Russian-speaking mechanic took me aside and pointed at some Soviet-built 2M62s and said to me in perfect English, "these machines are good locomotives". He was still proud of the old order.

Initially leaving Tallinn we were under wire, as the city's suburban services are an electrified operation. A few minutes out of Tallinn we passed a Soviet era electric train inbound. I'd travelled on these on my previous visit, and found them functional, but Spartan. Compared with the freight train their view was substandard. Unlike other former Soviet mainlines that are largely electrified, wires here are not for freight, the electrification ended outside of Tallinn's suburban district.

Tapa was the site of a vast marshalling yard. This was the first stop for my train, but it was also as far as I would go that day. After uncoupling, Vladimir used

Above: In July 2002, Eesti Raudtee imported rebuilt General Electric diesels from the United States for freight service. This former Union Pacific C36-7i was on one of its first revenue trips in Estonia and seen leading empty oil cars at Tapa on the way back to the Russian interchange at Narva.

the locomotive as a taxi to deliver me to the passenger station. Towards evening, my freight roared eastwards out of the yard, and Vladimir and his brakeman waved farewell to me.

The next morning, I returned to Tallinn on an intercity passenger train, then operated by Edelaraudtee. Later I rode another intercity passenger train to Viljandi. This was more comfortable than the train from Tapa. On the way we paused at Turi, where many passengers got off, while at Olustvere the train met a deluge.

As of 2014, Estonia's passenger trains have continued to operate, and in several area services have been improved. Long-distance services are operated by GoRail, with a daily train from Tallinn to St Petersburg, while several times a week an overnight sleeper train serves to Moscow. Domestic trains, now operated by Eesti Liinirongid—branded 'Elron,' connect Tallinn with outlying cities and towns. Recently, a coordinated service with Latvian railways, allows for a cross-border connection to Riga. Among the improvements are new trains to displace Soviet-era relics.

Left: The view from the cab of an Eesti Raudtee freight working east in suburban Tallinn. The overhead electrification was only used by Tallinn commuter trains; freights and long-distance passenger trains were diesel powered.

FINLAND
TO THE ARCTIC, FINNISH STYLE
North from Helsinki to the Land of the Midnight Sun

BRIAN SOLOMON

For the ardent train rider, Finland is one of the great unsung destinations. VR Group ('Valtionrautatiet' is the Finnish word meaning 'State Railways' and the initials 'VR' are typically used by the railway) offers excellent inter-

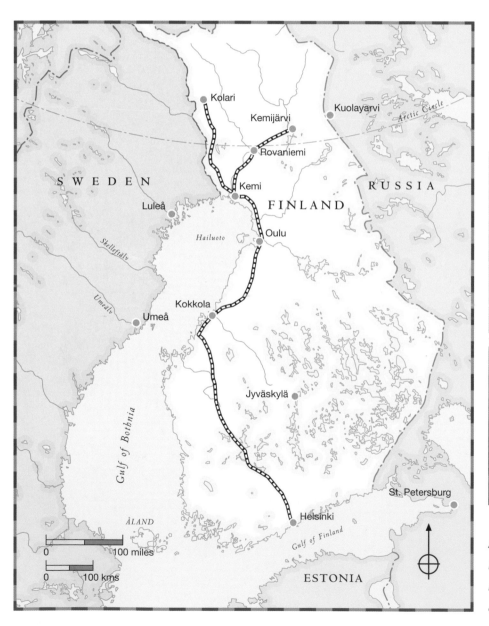

Above: Finland's railways enjoy a broad loading gauge as well as a broader than normal track gauge; as a result its passenger carriages are tall, spacious and comfortable.

city passenger services from the capital Helsinki to most outlying Finnish cities. Trains are maintained in top condition and the track is largely in textbook-perfect condition (except following the annual thaw when work is needed). VR continues to operate many traditional, locomotive-hauled trains, and its carriages are spacious and comfortable with large windows. Many intercity services carry dining cars that offer full meals, while overnight trains feature sleeping cars with a variety of accommodation, including single and double compartments. In addition, VR also runs modern, tilting, Italian-built Pendolino trains that operate in premier service.

Among the most exotic journeys are those from Helsinki to the northern regions. Two lines cross into the Lapland regions north of Arctic Circle, where in summer the famed midnight sun keeps the sky lit day and night, and in winter darkness reigns for weeks on end. Winter skies may exhibit the 'Northern Lights' or Aurora Borealis, a mesmerizing, scintillating, natural phenomenon caused by electrically charged solar particles colliding with atmospheric gases above the magnetic pole. Nocturnal displays can last from a few seconds to several minutes and at times light up the whole sky with cosmic, effervescent swirls.

Begin your Arctic rail journey in the Finnish capital, Helsinki. Located on the northern shore of the Gulf of Finland, Helsinki is a bustling metropolis with a variety of eclectic architecture and considerable railway interest. A classic urban tram system which hosts the distinctive, seasonal Spårakoff Pub Tram runs along the city streets. This easily identifiable red tram should be booked in advance during peak times as it can be very popular. Below ground Helsinki features a metro, while electrified commuter trains link the centre and the suburbs.

Above: Helsinki has a traditional city tram network where, in addition to regular service trams, tourists can avail themselves of the ever-popular Pub Tram which serves beer and cider as it circles the city. What better way to begin a trip to the Arctic than with a tour around the Finnish capital, drink in hand?

The star attraction for railway and architecture enthusiasts is Helsinki's main station, which is among the most famous and distinctive railway terminals in the world. Designed by one of Finland's greatest architects, Eliel Saarinen, construction began in 1905, but was delayed by the events of the First World War and not inaugurated until 1919, making it one of the last classic stations in Europe. Saarinen blended nationalistic elements with themes from the Arts & Crafts movement and traditional Finnish rural architecture. At the time, Finland was still dominated by the Russian empire and had embraced a nationalistic arts movement to counter Czarist influences. Its most identifiable features are exhibited on its front façade whose great portal archway is flanked by pairs of giant statues holding large globes.

Yet, Finland's railway network is a legacy of Russian domination. Not only are the tracks still based on Russian broad gauge (Finland's track gauge is 1,524 mm compared with Russia's 1,520 mm which is close enough to allow railway cars to use both lines), but the core network was laid out during Czarist times and Russia remains Finland's largest railway freight interchange. Today, Karelian Trains (with headquarters in Helsinki) is a joint venture between Finnish and Russian railways that operates deluxe, through passenger service between Helsinki and St Petersburg including dual-current electric Pendolino tilting trains on the *Allegro* service up to four times daily, plus an overnight service called the *Tolstoi* from Helsinki to Moscow.

Trains from Helsinki run north to the Arctic via Oulu, using one route to reach Rovaniemi and Kemijärvi, and another to reach Kolari. Although it's possible to take a through overnight train from Helsinki to Kemijärvi, this involves a 13-hour trip and unless made in the long days of summer will not allow passengers to see very much along the way. A better option is to make an Arctic journey in stages. Take the train to a midway point, such as Oulu, and spend the night there before continuing north.

Rovaniemi is located on the Arctic Circle, with its railway station south of the famous

Opposite: In the early 20th century, Finnish architect, Eliel Saarinen was inspired by the Vienna Secession movement, and blended elements of the Arts & Crafts movement with traditional Finnish themes in his romantic and nationalistic Helsinki Main Station.

Below: Finland's mainlines are now largely electrified and trains run from Helsinki to north of the Arctic Circle under wire. Against a textured northern sky, a VR Group class Sr2 electric leads a northbound passenger train at Oulu.

THE BERGEN AND FLÅM LINES
Through Tunnels and over Mountains to the Fjords

BRIAN SOLOMON

Norway is a sparsely populated, mostly rural country with unusually rugged geography and an exceptionally jagged coastline. Its seaside towns were linked to sea-trade and in the 19th century had little to gain from railway development, so its earliest lines were focused on inland routes. Today, while Norway's network remains relatively scant, it crosses famously difficult territory and offers some of the world's best travel experiences.

The Norge Statsbaner (Norwegian State Railways) Bergen Line connects the capital at Oslo (called Kristiana until 1925) with the southern coastal port at Bergen. As built, this route extended across 306 miles (484 km) of impossibly difficult terrain requiring clever engineering to cross a stunning Scandinavian landscape. The route follows a sinuous alignment involving countless rock cuttings and numerous tunnels. Today this route is famous for its tapestry of mountain landscapes, intermingled with river valleys, fjords and glaciers that place it among the world's most scenic train rides.

Ringed by mountain ranges, Bergen is the railway's western terminal and a picturesque port on the south side of the harbour on a coastal fjord. The railway station is just a short distance from the town's historic centre, famous for its fish

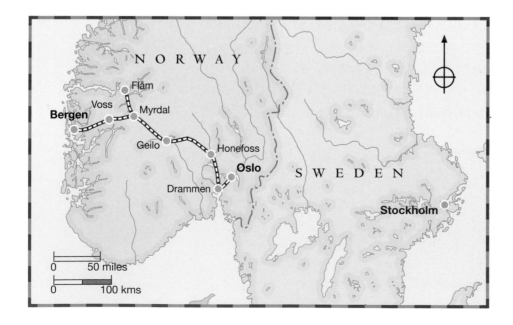

market and the Bryggen Hanseatic Wharf. Other attractions include the Fløibanen funicular railway. The railway running east of here towards the capital was built at various times. The westernmost 67-mile (108-km) section between Bergen and Voss was originally a narrow gauge route first opened to traffic in 1883. This line was carved into the face of vertical cliff sides or through them in tunnels. The eastern extension between Voss and Oslo was completed in 1909, built through upland regions, featuring 24 miles (38 km) of tunnel consisting of more than 180 individual bores. The longest is the $3\frac{1}{3}$-mile (5.3-km) Gravahals/Gravehalsen Tunnel.

Myrdal is a mountain enclave at the crossing of the Flåm Valley and a junction with the appropriately named Flåm Line. Beyond Myrdal, the Bergen route reaches a summit 4,200 feet (1,280 m) above sea level. From here it begins its long descent towards Oslo; on its final miles using a circuitous approach through thick Norwegian forest.

Travelling Norwegian Railways in Winter

Michael Walsh travelled the Bergen and Flåm lines in the dead of winter when Norway fulfills its legendary reputation as a land of ice and snow. Michael

Above: Railway attractions at Bergen include the Fløibanen funicular railway that climbs 1,050 feet (320 m) and offers stunning views of the surrounding fjords.

PORTUGAL
PORTUGUESE TRAMS
Rolling Antiques in Picturesque Urban Landscapes

BRIAN SOLOMON

Purists will be quick to point out that tram lines are distinctly different from heavy-rail railways. Yet both use tracks and railway vehicles, and Portugal's remarkable, historic, urban tramways are often considered among Europe's rail highlights. Lisbon's trams, in particular, are famous for their exceptional grades with trackage through narrow, ancient, winding streets and some of the most stunning urban views available from any rail-based vehicle. While both Lisbon and Porto once operated extensive electric tramway systems, these were radically paired back in favour of other modes. By the 1990s it appeared that Portuguese trams were facing oblivion, however both systems have survived and enjoyed limited revivals.

Portugal also operates a well-run intercity railway network. International sleeping-car trains using TALGO-built carriages connect Lisbon and Madrid, and Lisbon with the French frontier (see page 21). Like Spain, Portugal uses a wide Iberian track gauge, among the broadest in the world. There is a nominal difference in width (Portugal's is 1,664 mm to Spain's 1,668 mm), but this doesn't interfere with interchange and equipment can use the tracks of both railways. Among the most scenic of the heavy-rail routes is the line up the Douro Valley from Porto.

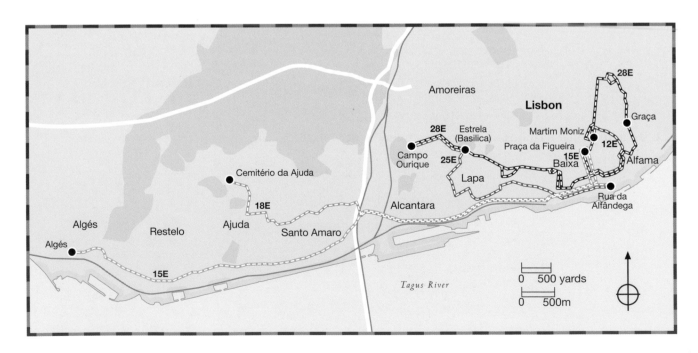

Lisbon's Trams

Built on the hills overlooking the Tagus estuary, at the western-most point in continental Europe, Lisbon is Portugal's capital and largest city. According to legend,
Lisbon was founded by the Greek hero Ulysses. Its oldest area is the famed Alfama district, characterized by narrow alleys and winding streets. In 1755, Lisbon
was destroyed by a tremendous earthquake which left little standing.

Historically, Portugal has enjoyed close ties with Britain, and one of the fruits
of this international relationship is the city's tramway network. This dates from
1873 and was owned by a British company in its formative years.

Tracks use a narrow gauge, just 2 feet 11⁷/₁₆ inches (900 mm) between the
rails, which permits some of the tightest urban trackage of any existing tram
system. Lisbon's route system was once extensive; surviving lines include some
of the most extreme examples of conventional electric tram construction in the
world, where lines skirt precariously close to buildings and around unusually
tight corners. In several places where a double line is impractical, interlace trackage is used, which limits operation to controlled single-line working to prevent
collisions. In other places single track operation with short passing sidings is

*Above: Lisbon's trams are often crammed
with passengers. A man flagging the 28
tram in an alley receives an apologetic
gesture from the driver.*

employed, meaning that cars in one direction must take a siding to get out of the way of cars travelling in the opposite direction.

Of surviving tramway routes, lines 25E and 28E feature some of the most interesting trackage and views. Line 28E is particularly interesting for tourists, since it winds through the historic Alfama and Graça districts where there are picture-postcard views at every turn. Line 12 makes a complete circuit over some of the same trackage as other routes but is a favourite with tourists aiming to explore the city.

Lisbon has renovated its historic tram fleet, and while the bodies of the cars retain the essential appearance of pre-Second World War, four-wheel trams, they have been modernized to make them more functional. Despite their antique appearance the tram routes are still operated as part of Lisbon's urban transportation system. They were featured in the 2013 film *Night Train to Lisbon* with Jeremy Irons. In the mid-1990s, new low-floor trams were bought for line 18, which skirts the waterfront and shares trackage with the older trams in the city centre. In addition to yellow-and-white service trams, there are special red trams that specifically cater to tourists.

One of the characteristics of Lisbon's tram system is its reputation for especially active pickpockets. While this is by no means a unique phenomenon to Lisbon, the scourge of tramway pickpockets must be considered when travelling. Understanding how these common thieves work should avoid most unpleasant encounters. Pickpockets tend to frequent tram terminals and other busy places where people, especially tourists, congregate and crowd together. When people are queueing to board trams, pickpockets will often work from behind by mingling with the crowd and pressing against victims. Protect yourself: keep valuables tucked away and watch for unwelcome bumps when queueing. Another pickpocket scam involves pairs working together: one of them will attempt to engage you in conversation, sometimes by asking the time of day, while his/her accomplice robs you. Despite the danger, don't let the threat of pickpockets deter you from your trip — Lisbon's trams are well worth a visit.

Above: Unusually steep trackage combined with narrow streets and eclectic architecture often result in comparisons between Lisbon's electrically powered trams and San Francisco's cable cars. Both are sun-tinged, antique, urban railway vehicles maintained for the benefit of tourists and operated as part of their city's transport system.

Opposite: Specially painted red trams cater to Lisbon tourists but intermingle with service trams in the city streets. A red tourist tram works dogleg trackage at Praça da Figueira.

Porto's Trams

Porto has two entirely separate tram networks, both with 4 foot 8½ inch (1,435 mm) standard gauge track. The first is a vestige of the historic system and uses preserved trams on select tourist routes in the city centre. Some of the vintage four-wheel trams are century-old, American-designed Brills, similar to the four-wheel trams that once worked many North American cities. The second is a modern system using low-floor cars on a metro-like light rail network, a portion of which is on the right-of-way of former steam-hauled, narrow gauge lines. While not an exotic journey, the modern system is interesting to ride and provides Porto with an excellent urban and suburban transport system. The highlight of the modern network is the crossing of the Douro on the famed Ponte Luis I (see pages 162-163) — an enormous steel arch bridge designed by Gustav Eiffel that bears a strong stylistic similarity to his famous Parisian tower.

Historic trams operate on three routes between March and November. Line 1 is a relatively long, riverfront route extending from Infante near the Museu dos Tranportes e Comunicaçöes (Museum of Transportation and Communications), to Porto Alegre, running beneath the massive Ponte Arrábida. Line 18 runs from a connection with line 1 near the Museu do Carro Eléctrico (Tram Museum) up some steeply inclined track making a loop near the city centre. Line 22 shares some trackage with line 18 at Carmo and makes a full loop through the city centre also on some steeply graded trackage. As well as these traditional adhesion tram lines, Porto has a precipitously steep funicular tram route that runs from the base of Ponte Luis I to a terminal near the end of line 22 at Guindais.

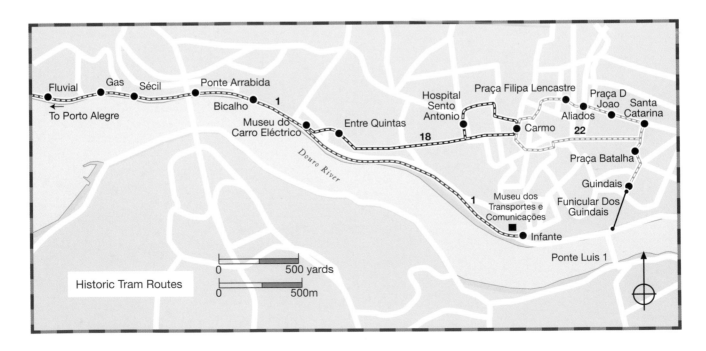

Above: *Porto's trams run on standard gauge (4 feet 8½ inch/1,435 mm) tracks. This is unusual in Portugal where the railways use either broad or narrow gauge tracks, and other tram systems are narrow gauge.*

Left: *Compared to Lisbon's trams, Porto's vintage cars retain their historic interiors. However, where in Lisbon vintage cars are operated as part of the public transit system, in Porto the cars are treated as a tourist excursion line.*

IRELAND
IRISH BRANCH LINES
It's a Long Way to Tipperary on Irish Rail

BRIAN SOLOMON

reland's first railway opened in December 1834, making the country one of the earliest, after England, to introduce passenger services that were primarily loco-motive hauled. The 6-mile (9.5-km) line connected Dublin with the harbour at Kingstown (today Dún Laoghaire). Curiously, while this first railway was built to the British standard gauge (4 feet 8½ inches/1,435 mm), Ireland's other early railways failed to settle on this standard and initially a variety of incompatible gauges came into use. The gauge disparity resulted in the Board of Trade mandat-ing a new standard in 1846; instead of adopting the 4 foot 8½ inch (1,435 mm) standard used by Ireland's pioneer Dublin & Kingstown Railway and by most lines in Britain, it opted for a novel solution by roughly averaging the gauges in use resulting in a broad 5 foot 3 inch (1,600 mm) gauge as the Irish standard. This awkward compromise not only remains in use to the present day, but was adopted in several other countries as well, notably Australia and Brazil.

By the end of the 19th century, railways connected most major Irish towns, with the most intensive networks focused on urban conurbations in Belfast, Cork and Dublin. In addition to its broad gauge network, from 1875 narrow gauge peripheral railways were built to link outlying points with connections to broad gauge lines. These light railways, as elsewhere around the world, cost less to build and could serve points beyond the practical reach of more heavily built lines. These were among Ireland's quaintest and most colourful lines and included such famous companies as the Tralee & Dingle, the West Clare and the Londonderry & Lough Swilly Railways. However, among the most curious of all Irish rural railways was the Listowel & Ballybunion line, built using the bizarre Lartigue monorail system.

By 1921, Irish railways reached their zenith at just over 3,440 route miles (5,537 km). However, the creation of the independent Irish state in 1922 and the partitioning of the six northern counties coincided with a long period of eco-nomic stagnation that was particularly cruel to the Irish railway network, which over the decades was gradually pruned back. Rural branch lines suffered the most. One by one, the quaint narrow gauge systems, once the delight of intrepid railway travellers, were all closed. The West Clare Railway survived the longest: it made its final run on 2 February 1961.

Consolidation resulted in a myriad other changes over the years, including the closing of many rural stations. In more recent times, massive investment in Irish railways during the Celtic Tiger economic boom had a two-fold effect of improving and increasing service, while marginalizing much of the historic character of surviving railways. Modernization can be equated with uglification of many traditional stations and facilities.

Despite decades of decline and modern changes, Irish railways continue to offer some eclectic and unusual journeys, vestiges of the earlier eras that may intrigue the intrepid traveller.

Dublin & South Eastern Route

Irish Rail operates railways in the Republic of Ireland, including Intercity, Commuter and Dublin Area Rapid Transit (DART) services. Among these lines is the Dublin & South Eastern route. This includes the original Dublin & Kingstown route, known as the world's first suburban railway, which was extended and connected with other lines in the mid-19th century to provide a through line from Dublin to Wexford and beyond to Rosslare Harbour (now Rosslare Europort). Ireland's island landmass has been compared to the shape of a teddy bear, and in this analogy, Rosslare is at the teddy bear's tail.

Historically, the Dublin & South Eastern route began at the station in Westland Row (Pearse Station since 1966). This was opened in 1834, giving it the claim to be the oldest city terminal in continuous use in the world. In 1891, it was linked with Amiens Street Station on Dublin's North Side via the elevated loop line. DART electric trains use the line as far as Greystones in County Wicklow. While a journey on the DART south from Connolly will provide some of the finest views of any commuter line in Europe, the less frequent Intercity trains to Rosslare are a more comfortable choice.

Near Booterstown, a few miles south of Dublin, the line joins the shore of the Irish Sea. Here the tracks follow the 1834 alignment, and the seawall between the railway and beach is partially constructed from Dublin & Kingstown's original stone sleepers. From Dún Laoghaire the line turns inland, running through a deep cutting and angling towards Dalkey. Beyond Dalkey is a short curved tunnel, and, when the line emerges again, it descends on a shelf high above the Irish Sea towards Killiney. On a sunny morning there is a captivating view of the scintillating blue sea from the train as it glides down the grade towards Killiney Beach.

Bray is a Victorian seaside resort town and a DART terminal where trains are stored between runs. Beyond Bray, the line climbs around Bray Head, diving through a series of tunnels, and passes Brandy Hole, the site of a famous train wreck in the 1860s that landed passenger cars in the water and on the rocks far below the line. But, fear not modern traveller! Since that unfortunate mishap, resourceful railway engineers have carved out a superior route, and the present line is safely inland from the original route (hence the need for additional tunnels).

The DART service and the overhead wires that power it only go as far as Greystones, but the railway continues. Miles of seaside running extend to Wicklow, but here the line again turns inland. At Rathdrum the line descends through a tunnel and emerges to pass the Vale of Avoca. While the scenery remains pleasant for the rest of the journey down the South Eastern route, the most impressive scenery is in the first hour of travel. Beyond the station at Wexford town, one of several communities along the line founded by the Vikings more than a

millennium ago, the railway nimbly navigates road-side trackage along Wexford Quay. The town is on the right side of the train. Rosslare Strand is a junction where the now-disused line to Waterford via Wellington Bridge diverges. The stretch of seaside running between Wexford and Rosslare Harbour presents more than just pretty vistas: the threat of rising sea-levels present long-term problems from erosion that someday may result in closure of the line.

Above: Among Irish Rail's scenic highlights are the views of the Irish Sea between Dalkey and Wicklow. A Dublin-Rosslare intercity train exits the Dalkey tunnel in the area colloquially known as 'the Irish Riviera'.

Tipperary Branches

The iconic First World War song, *It's a long way to Tipperary*, seems to have special relevance to the Irish Rail branches across the midlands county. Although these remain some of most intriguing railway lines in Ireland, the track speeds are slow and it seems to take an age to get from one end of the line to the other. But that's part of the charm. Taking a spin on these out-of-the-way lines is about the experience, not about getting to the end of the line. One of the unusual characteristics of both long Tipperary branches is that they connect with other active rail routes at both ends, so where Irish mainlines are large stub-end routes, the branches are not, which is, of course, quite the opposite of what is expected of a branch, and allows travellers the ability to make circular trips without having to return on the same line. These branches, like so many charming Irish railways, are underappreciated and seem to be perpetually under threat.

Both the Nenagh Branch (from Ballybrophy to Limerick) and the Waterford to Limerick Junction line retain classic Victorian-era signalling. Here in traditional signal cabins, like those found on preserved railways, signalmen maintain the old order, communicating to one another using telegraphic instruments, and

Above: The view of Dublin's Custom House as seen crossing the Loop Line on a Railway Preservation Society Ireland trip to Wicklow. This once-controversial bridge (some Victorians protested at what they deemed its unsightly qualities) is one of the most important railway links in Dublin and key to modern DART and Intercity services.

setting points and signals using mechanical interlocked levers. While one of the oldest methods of signalling, this is also recognized as one of the safest. When paused at Roscrea or Birdhill on the Nenagh Branch, listen for the bells in the cabin. These are communication codes between signalmen. Then watch for the signalman who will pass a metal staff to the train driver that authorizes the train to proceed. Under the normal rules, every train must have a staff to enter a section, and one and only one staff can be issued for each specific section as defined in the timetable.

Above: Railway Preservation Society Ireland's engine 186 leads an excursion on the Dublin & South Eastern route at Dalkey. Number 186 is a class J15 0-6-0 built in 1879 by Sharp, Stewart & Company in Manchester, England. In its day, the J15 was a common locomotive on many Irish branch lines. RPSI operates dozens of stream trips annually on Irish railways.

To Sligo on the Old Midland Route

Traditionally, Midland Great Western Railway (MGWR) served Dublin via an elegant, if awkwardly located, terminal at Broadstone on the city's north side, near the King's Inn. The railway established its Dublin terminal adjacent to the Royal canal basin. Broadstone's passenger station features neo-Egyptian style architecture.

In the 1920s, the new Irish Government encouraged an amalgamation of companies in the south that grouped the old D&SE, Great Southern & Western Railway and MGWR into the new Great Southern Railways in 1925. Passenger services from Dublin's Broadstone were shifted to Westland Row in 1937. Now if you want to board a train for Sligo, you do so from Dublin's Connolly Station. Broadstone survived as a steam depot until the end of the steam era in the 1960s. Rails were lifted in the 1970s, yet the structure remains and functions ignominiously as the headquarters and main depot for Bus Éireann. Soon, tracks will return, as a new tram line extending from Dublin's Stephen's Green to Broombridge will follow the old Midland right-of-way north of Broadstone.

Take the train to Sligo and enjoy the former Midland line as works its way west along the Royal Canal towards Mullingar. In places you'll see the old locks and you may even witness the passage of a boat, although this remains a relatively

Above: Twice daily, Irish Rail operates a local service on the Nenagh Branch between Ballybrophy and Limerick. On a summer morning, a Limerick-bound 2800-series diesel railcar approaches the station at Roscrea, County Tipperary. A classic signal cabin that controls signalling in the station is on the left.

rare event. The Midland route retained active signal cabins until 2005, when the line was converted to a modern colour light signalling system controlled from Dublin. Yet the old cabins can be seen at various points, including near the station at Enfield, at the closed station in Killucan, at Mullingar and Sligo.

In its heyday, Mullingar was an important junction and a hub for cattle traffic. Tracks reached here in October 1848, and were soon extended west towards Galway. Later the Sligo line was built, branching off the Galway route here, and reaching its namesake in 1862. Mullingar Station sits between the two lines, with the old cabin perched high on the Dublin end of the platform. The Galway side of the station is largely derelict. Except for annual steam excursions and the occasional permanent way (maintenance) train, nothing uses these tracks nor can trains continue beyond Mullingar on the Galway line. Although once a busy main route, the last movement over the line occurred in May 2003, when a weed-spraying train made one final pass. The tracks remain, buried beneath the undergrowth. To reach Galway, Irish Rail now uses another route via Portarlington and Clara to Athlone, where trains rejoin the old Midland route.

The ride from Mullingar to Sligo is pleasant and pastoral. At Sligo there are memorable views of Benbulben, a mesa-like landmass memorialized in verse by W. B. Yeats.

Below: Ireland has many wonderful 19th-century railway stations. A Dublin-bound Irish Rail Rotem railcar arrives at Mullingar. The modern train offers a contrast to the traditional platform canopies and classic stone station.

Steam and Rail Tours

Irish Rail operates multiple trips daily on all intercity routes, including branches. Most trains consist of modern, Korean-built Rotem diesel railcars, which provide comfortable seating, feature tables between facing sets of seats and large windows to view the scenery. However, a more interesting way to travel is via specially organized tours with vintage equipment.

The Railway Preservation Society Ireland maintains authentic Irish steam locomotives and traditional carriages for periodic excursions. Among its most popular regular runs are trips on the Dublin & South Eastern route and to Mullingar on the Midland. Select Irish Rail crews have been specially trained to work steam locomotives and maintain the old knowledge passed down by generations of railway men. Keeping these locomotives in running order requires lots of work, while operating them on active lines takes skill. Listen to the exhaust of

Below: A Railway Preservation Society Ireland steam special works the Nenagh Branch at Shalee, County Tipperary. Locomotive number 4 is a tank engine built in 1947 for Belfast suburban service and is one of several steam locomotives maintained by the RPSI.

engine 461 as it climbs up Glenealy Bank south of Wicklow, or gains speed along the Midland line west of Enfield. These are the sounds of railways as they were nearly a century ago.

Railtours Ireland First Class is a Dublin-based tour company specializing in railway-based tourism. It offers a variety of tours including an annual eight-day, first-class *Emerald Isle Express* tour that covers many of Ireland's most interesting branch line railways. Belmond, operators of British Pullman and *Venice Simplon-Orient-Express*, anticipates operating its new *Belmond Grand Hibernian* in 2016. This is expected to consist of two-, four- and six-night luxury rail tours to major destinations in both the Republic of Ireland and Northern Ireland.

Above: The old Midland Great Western Railway route offers classic views of rural Ireland. Locomotive 461 leads a Railway Preservation Society Ireland excursion eastwards along the Royal Canal near Enfield.

RESOURCES

Railway websites

Alaska Railroad: www.alaskarailroad.com

Australia: for Hotham Valley: www.hothamvalleyrailway.com.au/

for long-distance passenger trains: www.transwa.wa.gov.au/

for the West Coast Wilderness Railway: www.wcwr.com.au or www.greatrailexperiencestasmania.com.au

for mainline trains, Western Australia: www.wa.gov.au/

for the Great Southern Railway: www.greatsouthernrail.com.au

Bolivia: Andean railways', Empressa Ferroviaria Andina (FCA), website offers up-to-date information, (however as of 2015 this was entirely in Spanish) : www.fca.com.bo/subcontenido.

for current Bolivian railway schedules: www.fahrplancenter.com/

Chile: for schedules see EFE's website: www.tmsa.cl/link.cgi/

European Railway schedules: see Germany's Deutsche Bahn website, which provides information that is easy and logical to navigate: reiseauskunft.bahn.de/

Finland: VR's website: www.vr.fi

Hokkaido's local trains: en.visit-hokkaido.jp/access/transportation/rails

Ireland: for regularly scheduled trains, tickets and news: www.irishrail.ie

RPSI trips: www.steamtrainsireland.com/events/

Railtours Ireland: www.railtoursireland.com

Belmond: www.belmond.com

Malaysia: North Borneo Railway: www.northborneorailway.com.my

Sabah State Railway: www.railway.sabah.gov.my

Moroccan railways: Office National des Chemins de Fer du Maroc (ONCF): www.oncf.ma/

Norway: for schedules and fares: www.nsb.no/en/our-destinations/

Orient Express: www.belmond.com/venice-simplon-orient-express/journeys/

South Shore: for schedules and up-to-date information: www.nictd.com

Spanish railways: www.renfe.com/EN/viajeros/

Spain to Morocco ferry services, see FRS: www.frs.es/en/

Peru: for timetables and fares for the *Andean Explorer*: www.perurail.com/andean-explorer

for Belmond's PeruRail trips: www.perurail.com/

for Inca Rail timetables and fares: www.incarail.com/machupicchu

Portugal's national railway, Combros de Portugal: www.cp.pt/

Quebec: see TRT's website for current information: www.tshiuetin.net/

Thailand/Malaysia: for information on the *Eastern & Oriental Express*: www.belmond.com

KTM Berhad: www.ktmb.com.my and the State Railways of Thailand: www.railway.co.th

Vietnam Railways: vietnam-railway.com/

Zimbabwe: Victoria Falls Steam Train Company: www.steamtraincompany.com

Reading

Faith, N. and Wolmar, C. (2014). *The World the Railways Made*. Head of Zeus

Harlow, A. (1947). *Road of the Century*. Creative Age Press

Malik, M. B. K. (1962). *A Hundred Years of Pakistan Railways*. Govt of Pakistan

Miller, C. (1972). *Lunatic Express*. Macdonald

Peterson, Col. J. H. (1908, re-issued 2014). *The Man-eaters of Tsavo*. CreasteSpace Independent Publishing Platform

Theroux, P. (1975, republished 2008 by Penguin) *The Great Railway Bazaar*. Houghton Mifflin

Acknowledgements

The preparation of this book involved the experiences, recollections and photography of many seasoned railway travellers. Special thanks to Paul Bigland, David Bowden and Scott Lothes for their written contributions.

Michael Walsh is an intrepid traveller with an unusual wide breadth of experience. He was especially gracious and supplied material from many countries from the Americas to Asia, Australia and Europe. Thanks to Stephen Hirsh and Denis McCabe for their assistance with a variety of Russian and Asian experiences, include the Trans-Siberian and Trans-Mongolian journeys. Mark Healy assisted with Kenya. Oliver Doyle lent perspective and knowledge helpful during this book's early preparatory stages. Donncha Cronin assisted with Cuba and Asia. Tom Carver helped with Adirondack Scenic and Quebec, North Shore & Labrador. John Brahaney helped with viewpoints on the Alaska Railroad. Markku Pulkkinen assisted me with my travels in Finland and assisted with proofreading my Finnish text. Ed Burkhardt, Tom Tancula and the members of Eesti Raudtee staff facilitated my travels in Estonia. Thanks to Mike Abalos, Mike Danneman and Chris Guss for tours of the South Shore.

Ken Fox, Pat Yough, Tim Doherty, Hassard Stackpoole, David Hegarty, Gerry Conmy, Peter Rigney, Norman Gamble, Tim Moriarty, Alan Hyland, Dan Smith, Railtours Ireland First Class's Jim Deegan, Tom Hargadon, Clark Johnson Jr., and Steve Carlson variously assisted by making introductions, lending research materials or photographs, or advised me on their travel experiences.

Thanks to Colm O'Callaghan, Chris Southwell, Jack Wright, Petri Tuovinen, Belmond's Hannah Layton, Samantha Strawford and Gemma Cánepa, and Tren Ecuador's Daniela Guarderas and Slav Ivanov for helping with illustrations.

My father Richard J. Solomon introduced me to railways at a very young age and has travelled with me on many railway trips in North America, Europe and Japan. He lent the use of his library, travel expertise, photographic collection and helped with proofreading.

Special thanks to Rosemary Wilkinson and John Beaufoy without whom this book could not have been possible.

INDEX

First published in the United Kingdom in 2015 by John Beaufoy Publishing,
11 Blenheim Court, 316 Woodstock Road, Oxford OX2 7NS, England www.johnbeaufoy.com

10 9 8 7 6 5 4 3 2 1

ISBN 978-1-909612-17-4

Designed by Glyn Bridgewater Cartography by William Smuts Project management by Rosemary Wilkinson

Printed and bound in Malaysia by Times Offset (M) Sdn Bhd

Photo credits Belmond 7, 12, 13, 120, 121; Paul Bigland 41, 53, 54, 55; David Bowden 1, 62, 63, 64, 65, 66, 67, 68, 69, 70, 71, 72, 73, 135, 136, 137, 153, 154, 155, 156, 157, 159; Tom Carver 81, 83; Donncha Cronin 108, 109, 110, 111; Graham Duro 34-5; Great Southern Rail 5, 159, 161; Mark Healy 139, 141; Stephen Hirsch 25; Scott Lothes 43, 44, 46, 47, 49, 50, 51, 56, 58, 59, 60, 61; Denis McCabe 23, 28, 29, 30, 31, 32, 33; Colm O'Callaghan 101, 102, 103 (top), 104, 105, 106; PeruRail 112-3, 119; Shutterstock.com/Ami Parikh 74-5, rory cummins 26-7, russal 8-9, serjio74 2-3; Brian Solomon 14, 15, 16, 17, 19, 20, 21, 85, 87, 88, 89, 91, 92, 93, 95, 97, 98, 99 (bottom), 162-3, 165, 166, 167, 169, 170, 171, 172, 174, 175, 176, 177, 178, 179, 180, 181, 183 (top), 189, 190, 191, 193, 197, 198, 199, 200, 201, 202, 203; Richard J. Solomon 94, 99 (top); Chris Southwell 77, 79; Tren Ecuador/David Grijalva 129, 131, 132, 133; Visit-Bergen - Visitnorway.com/Pål Hoff 185; Visit Flåm/Rolf M. Sørensen 186, Petri Tuovinen 182, 183 (bottom), E. A. Vikesland 187; Michael Walsh 37, 38, 39, 103 (bottom), 107, 115, 116, 117, 123, 125, 126, 127, 143, 144, 145, 146, 147, 149, 151; Jack Wright 82.